*Rings and
Homology*

Athena Series

SELECTED TOPICS IN MATHEMATICS

Edwin Hewitt, *Editor*

AMBROSE, LAZEROWITZ: LOGIC: THE THEORY OF FORMAL INFERENCE

BELLMAN: A BRIEF INTRODUCTION TO THETA FUNCTIONS

BELLMAN: PERTURBATION TECHNIQUES IN MATHEMATICS, PHYSICS, AND ENGINEERING

CARDANO: THE BOOK ON GAMES OF CHANCE

ERDÉLYI: OPERATIONAL CALCULUS AND GENERALIZED FUNCTIONS

FICKEN: THE SIMPLEX METHOD OF LINEAR PROGRAMMING

HADWIGER, DEBRUNNER, AND KLEE: COMBINATORIAL GEOMETRY IN THE PLANE

HEINS: SELECTED TOPICS IN THE CLASSICAL THEORY OF FUNCTIONS OF A COMPLEX VARIABLE

HIRSCHMAN: INFINITE SERIES

HOCHSTADT: SPECIAL FUNCTIONS OF MATHEMATICAL PHYSICS

JANS: RINGS AND HOMOLOGY

KAZARINOFF: ANALYTIC INEQUALITIES

WILLIAMSON: LEBESGUE INTEGRATION

James P. Jans

University of Washington

Rings and Homology

HOLT, RINEHART AND WINSTON

New York, Chicago, San Francisco
Toronto, London

Preface

This monograph was designed as an introduction to rings and homology that could be read by any student familiar with the very minimum of algebra. The idea was to mix a little ring structure with some homological algebra and give the student practice in the techniques of each area.

The first chapter contains definitions and standard material known to most first-year graduate students. The reader with some degree of mathematical maturity would do well to skip it and return to it when necessary. Chapter 2 is devoted largely to ring structure, in particular to the structure of semisimple rings with minimum condition. The exercises at the end of Chapter 2 are used to develop some of the theory of non-semisimple rings.

In Chapter 3 we develop certain elementary homological theory and use this to introduce the functor Ext. This machinery is used in Chapters 4 and 5 to study the various projective dimensions, global dimension, and duality theory.

At the end of each chapter we have included exercises that are designed to give the student practice in the theory developed in the chapter. In some cases we have used the exercises to carry the theory a bit farther. Indeed, a critical step in a proof in Chapter 5 rests on some properties of rings with minimum condition developed in the exercises at the end of Chapter 2. We strongly urge the reader to do the exercises as he goes along.

Naturally, there is a great deal of material that would not fit into a small monograph. For instance, some of our homological colleagues may miss their old friends, Tor and the tensor product. We found that in the dimension and duality theory, they were needed in only a few places and could be eliminated by the judicious use of lots of homs and Exts. We feel that we have included enough material for a one-semester or two-quarter course on rings and homology. The instructor can finish off the year with material of his own choice.

We should like to express our gratitude to J. W. Armstrong, with whom we collaborated on an earlier version of this monograph, and to H. Mochizuki and Eileen Wu for their interest in the subject and for their suggestions which improved the presentation at many points.

J. P. J.

December, 1963
Seattle, Washington

Contents

Preface   v

1. Basic Concepts   1
Schur's Lemma   4
Another Version of Schur's Lemma   4

2. Everybody Splits   12
Structure Theorem for Semisimple Rings with Minimum Condition   12
First Uniqueness Theorem   19
Second Uniqueness Theorem   21

3. Complexes, Homology, and Ext   27
The Exact Sequence of Homology Theorem   28
Theorem (Splitting of Ext)   43

4. Various Dimensions   47
The Shifting Theorem   47
The Dimension Theorem   48
Injective Producing Lemma   52
Shifting Theorem for Injectives   54
The Injective Dimension Theorem   55
Global Dimension Theorem   55

5. Duality and Quasi-Frobenius Rings   65
Third Dual Theorem   67
Some Properties of Torsionless Modules   67
Torsionless and Dual Theorem   69
References   83

Index   85

(1)

Basic Concepts

This chapter has been included to broaden the audience for this book to anyone who knows the definitions and elementary properties of rings, fields, and groups. Readers with a greater degree of mathematical maturity may skip this chapter and refer back to it when necessary.

DEFINITION. If R is an associative ring with an identity 1, then an (additive) abelian group M is called an *R-left module*, provided there is a unique element $ra \in M$, corresponding to each $r \in R$ and $a \in M$, such that

$$r(a + b) = ra + rb, \tag{1.1}$$

$$(rs)(a) = r(sa), \tag{1.2}$$

$$(r + s)(a) = ra + sa, \tag{1.3}$$

and

$$1a = a, \tag{1.4}$$

for all $r, s \in R$ and $a, b \in M$. The element ra is sometimes called the module product of r and a. For convenience, we shall refer to R-left modules as R modules.

Note that we put the ring elements on the left because of Eq. (1.2), which states that the product rs acts on M as "first s, then r." For commutative rings, this distinction is not important; the ring elements may be placed on whichever side of the module that is convenient. However, for noncommutative rings, a little more care is necessary.

An R right module S is defined analogously, with the module product designated by ar for a in S and r in R. Equation (1.2) becomes, in this case,

$$a(rs) = (ar)s \tag{1.2$'$}$$

which means that rs acts as "first r, then s."

EXAMPLES

1. Every abelian group is an R module, where R is the ring Z of integers.

2. Every vector space is an R module, where R is the base field of the vector space.

1

3. If R is a ring and B is a left (right) ideal, then B is an R module (right R module).

Suppose that M is an R module; then the set $I = \{r | rm = 0, \text{ all } m \in M\}$, is a two-sided ideal of R called the annihilator of M. If J is any two-sided ideal contained in I, then for any element j in J, we have $jM = 0$. Therefore, every element of the coset $r + J$ in R/J acts on M exactly as r does, and we can consider M as an R/J module by the definition $(r + J)m = rm$. The process sketched above can be reversed. If T is an R/S module, for S an ideal of R, then we can consider T as an R module by defining $rt = (r + S)t$ for $r \in R, t \in T$.

DEFINITION. If S is a subset of the R module M, then S is called an R *submodule of M* if S is a subgroup of M such that, for each $r \in R$, $\{rs | s \in S\} = rS \subseteq S$. If S is an R submodule of M, then the quotient group M/S is an R module with module multiplication given by $r(m + S) = rm + S$. The R module M/S is called the *quotient (factor) module of M by S*.

We shall say that an R module S is *simple* if it has exactly two R submodules, (0) and S.

If T_β is any collection of R submodules of an R module M, then $\cap T_\beta$ is also an R submodule. If T is a subset of M, then there exists a unique smallest R submodule M_T of M containing T. One way to get M_T is to form $\cap T_\beta$, where the T_β are all the R submodules of M containing the set T. Another way to get M_T is to take for M_T the set

$$\{\overset{f}{\textstyle\sum} r_i t_i \mid t_i \in T, r_i \in R\},$$

where the f over the $\sum$ indicates finite sum. The reader may check to see that both methods give rise to the same submodule M_T.

We shall say that T *generates* M if $M_T = M$. In the case that T is finite and $M = M_T$, we say that M is *finitely generated*. If M can be generated with one element, then we say that M is *cyclic*. When T is a set with one element t, we note that $M_t = Rt = \{rt | r \in R\}$. In the case $T = \cup S_\alpha$, S_α, an R submodule of M, the usual notation for M_T is $\sum S_\alpha$.

DEFINITION. Suppose that M and T are R modules and that f is a function from M into T:

$$f: M \to T;$$

then f is called an R *homomorphism* if f is a homomorphism of the additive group of M into the additive group of T, and if f satisfies the condition

$$f(rm) = rf(m), \quad r \in R, \quad m \in M.$$

The *kernel of f*, $\operatorname{Ker} f = \{m \in M | f(m) = 0\}$, and the *image of f*, $\operatorname{Im} f = \{f(m) \in T | m \in M\}$, are R submodules of M and T, respectively. If S is an R submodule of M, then there is a natural R homomorphism:

$$v: M \to M/S,$$

such that $\operatorname{Ker} v = S$ and $\operatorname{Im} v = M/S$. In fact,

$$v(m) = m + S, \quad m \in M.$$

An R homomorphism $f: M \to T$ is called an R *epimorphism*, R *monomorphism*, or R *isomorphism*, according as $\operatorname{Im} f = T$, $\operatorname{Ker} f = (0)$, or $\operatorname{Im} f = T$ and $\operatorname{Ker} f = (0)$, respectively. In the following discussion, we shall often use the terms "map" or "mapping" for R homomorphism because they are shorter.

There are a number of techniques for constructing new homomorphisms from old. We outline a few of these below.

If $f: M \to T$ in an R homomorphism and if $X \subseteq M$, $Y \subseteq T$, X, Y, submodules of M, T, respectively, with the property that $f(X) = \{f(x)|x \in X\} \subseteq Y$, then there is a new homomorphism $f': M/X \to T/Y$ given by $f'(m + X) = f(m) + Y$. One checks to see that the definition of f' applied to a coset is independent of the representative m of that coset and that f' is an R homomorphism. The homomorphism f' is said to be induced by f. Certain special cases of this technique for making new homomorphisms are of interest. For instance, let $X = \operatorname{Ker} f$, $Y = (0)$; in this case, the induced homomorphism $f': M/\operatorname{Ker} f \to T = T/(0)$ is actually a monomorphism.

Another process for inducing homomorphisms is as follows: If $f: M/X \to C$ is a homomorphism, then this induces $f'': M \to C$ where $f''(m) = f(m + X)$. One checks to see that this is a homomorphism and that $(f'')': M/X \to C$ is actually the same as $f: M/X \to C$, where $(\ )'$ indicates the process described before.

There are more obvious methods for constructing homomorphisms. If $f: M \to C$ is a homomorphism and if $X \subseteq M$, $Y \subseteq C$ such that $f(X) \subset Y$, then $f|X: X \to Y$ is also a homomorphism where $f|X$ is "f restricted to X." A special case of this occurs when $X = M$, and $Y = \operatorname{Im} f$. In this case $f: M \to \operatorname{Im} f$ is an epimorphism.

Some people occasionally confuse $f: M \to C$ with $f: M \to \operatorname{Im} f$. We shall try to avoid this by thinking of the homomorphism as a triple $f: M \to C$ consisting of two modules M, C, and a function f from M to C satisfying certain conditions. To say that two homomorphisms $f: M \to C$ and $g: N \to D$ are equal will mean that $M = N$, $C = D$, and $f(x) = g(x)$ for all $x \in M = N$. Sometimes the notation for this gets cumbersome, and we shall lapse into saying "the homomorphism f," although we should say the homomorphism $f: M \to C$.

When we have a simple R module and consider R homomorphisms in and out of it, we see that there are not very many possibilities for kernels and images. These facts are summed up in the following lemma.

Schur's Lemma   If S is simple, then a map out of S is either the zero map or is an R monomorphism, a map into S is either the zero map or an R epimorphism, and a map of S to itself is either the zero map or an R isomorphism.

If we have two R homomorphisms, $f: M \to T$ and $g: T' \to Q$, and if T is a submodule of T', then their composition $gf: M \to Q$ is also an R homomorphism. If the R homomorphisms are going in opposite directions, $h: A \to B$ and $k: B \to A$, we shall say that h and k are inverses of each other if hk is the identity function on A and kh is the identity function on B. In this case, it is easy to see that both h and k are R isomorphisms. Conversely, if h is an R isomorphism, then there exists a unique k such that h and k are inverses. These facts about isomorphisms, together with the easily verified property that the composition of isomorphisms in an isomorphism leads us to observe that "isomorphism is an equivalence relation." That is, we say $A \cong B$ if there exists $f: A \to B$, an R isomorphism. We shall often use the letter i for the identity isomorphism of a module on itself. Sometimes, where confusion is likely to occur, we shall add a subscript to indicate which module (that is, i_A is identity on A).

We can also add R homomorphisms. If $f: A \to B$ and $g: A \to B$ are R homomorphisms, then we define $f + g: A \to B$ by the rule $(f + g)(x) = f(x) + g(x)$, and it turns out that $f + g$ is an R homomorphism.

The reader can check quite easily that the set of all R homomorphisms of an R module to itself forms a ring where the multiplication is composition and the addition is the addition defined above.

Another Version of Schur's Lemma   If S is a simple R module, then the ring of all R homomorphisms of S to itself is a division ring.

A *division ring* (sometimes called a *field*) satisfies all the conditions for a field except that it need not be commutative. The second version of Schur's lemma follows from the first, since the nonzero R homomorphisms of S to itself must all have inverses.

In the following discussion we shall describe two methods of constructing new modules from old ones.

DEFINITION.   Let $\{M_\alpha\}\alpha \in \mathcal{A}$ be a collection of R modules indexed by a set $\mathcal{A}$; the *Cartesian product* (or *product*) $\Pi_\alpha M_\alpha$ is $\{f | f: \mathcal{A} \to \cup_\alpha M_\alpha, f(\alpha) \in M_\alpha\}$. We make $\Pi_\alpha M_\alpha$ into an R module by defining $rf(\alpha) = r(f(\alpha))$ and $(f + g)(\alpha) = f(\alpha) + g(\alpha)$.

There is a submodule $\oplus \sum_\alpha M_\alpha$ of $\Pi_\alpha M$ where

$$\oplus \sum_\alpha M = \left\{ f \middle| f \in \prod_\alpha M_\alpha \text{ and } f(\alpha) = 0 \quad \begin{array}{l} \text{for all but a} \\ \text{finite number of } \alpha \end{array} \right\}.$$

$\oplus \sum_\alpha M_\alpha$ is called the *direct sum* of the M_α. If the index set is finite, of course then $\oplus \sum_\alpha M_\alpha = \prod_\alpha M_\alpha$.

The direct sum and product are hooked up with homomorphisms in the following way: If $g_\alpha: B \to M_\alpha$ is a map from B to M_α for each α, then we can define $\prod_\alpha g_\alpha: B \to \prod_\alpha M_\alpha$, where $\prod_\alpha g_\alpha(b)$ is that function f in $\prod_\alpha M_\alpha$ with the property that $f(\alpha) = g_\alpha(b)$. One checks to see that $\prod_\alpha g_\alpha$ is an R homomorphism.

If we have maps $h_\alpha: M_\alpha \to C$ for each α, then we can define $\sum h_\alpha$: $\oplus \sum_\alpha M_\alpha \to C$ by the equation $\sum h_\alpha(f) = \sum_\alpha h_\alpha(f(\alpha))$, the latter being only a finite sum, since $f \in \sum_\alpha M_\alpha$ means $f(\alpha) = 0$ except for a finite number of α.

We shall not use the product very much, but we shall use the direct sum constantly. If someone produces a module, it is useful to have a method for determining whether it is a direct sum. In what follows we shall describe such a method. If M is a module with a collection of submodules $\{M_\alpha\} \alpha \in \mathcal{Q}$ satisfying the following conditions:

(1) $\sum_\alpha M_\alpha = M$ (that is, the set $\cup M_\alpha$ generates M),

(2)   For each α, $M_\alpha \cap \sum_{\beta \neq \alpha} M_\beta = (0)$,

then M is isomorphic to $\oplus \sum_\alpha M_\alpha$. The collection $\{M_\alpha\} \alpha \in \mathcal{Q}$ is called an *independent family* of submodules if it satisfies the condition (2). The isomorphism $\theta: \oplus \sum_\alpha M_\alpha \to M$ is given by the formula $\theta(f) = \sum_\alpha f(\alpha)$, the latter being only a finite sum. Property (1) above shows that θ is an epimorphism, and (2) implies that θ is a monomorphism. In case we have such a situation, we call the submodules M_α *direct summands* of M.

In the case that we have only a finite set of R modules $M_i, i = 1, 2, \ldots, n$, we may write their direct sum $\sum M_i = M_1 \oplus M_2 \oplus \ldots \oplus M_n$. The reader may check to see that the following isomorphisms hold:

$$M_1 \oplus M_2 \cong M_2 \oplus M_1,$$

$$M_1 \oplus (M_2 \oplus M_3) \cong (M_1 \oplus M_2) \oplus M_3 \cong M_1 \oplus M_2 \oplus M_3.$$

The last isomorphism says that "a direct summand of a direct summand is a direct summand," which will be of some use to us.

In the case of two summands M_1 and M_2, it is common to think of $M_1 \oplus M_2$ as $\{(x, y) | x \in M_1, y \in M_2\}$, where the addition and ring operation take place componentwise. It is clear that this coincides with our definition.

There are certain special homomorphisms into and out of $\oplus \sum_\alpha M_\alpha$ and $\prod_\alpha M_\alpha$. For a fixed index α_0, define $p_{\alpha_0}: \prod_\alpha M_\alpha \to M_{\alpha_0}$ by the equation $p_{\alpha_0}(f) = f(\alpha_0)$; p_{α_0} is called the *projection on the α_0 coordinate*. There is also a mapping into the product $j_{\alpha_0}: M_{\alpha_0} \to \prod_\alpha M_\alpha$, where $j_{\alpha_0}(m)$ is that function f

in $\Pi_\alpha M_\alpha$ with the property that $f(\alpha_0) = m$ and $f(\alpha) = 0$ for $\alpha \neq \alpha_0$. Note that $p_{\alpha_0} j_{\alpha_0}$ is identity on M_{α_0}, which shows that p_{α_0} is an epimorphism and t_{α_0} is a monomorphism. The same formulas are used to define projections out of the direct sum and injections into it. We shall think of M_{α_0} as being a submodule of the product and sum because it is isomorphic to $\operatorname{Im} j_{\alpha_0}$, which is a submodule of the product and sum.

DEFINITION. Suppose $\{M_i\}$ is a nonempty collection of R modules with a corresponding collection of mappings $f_i: M_i \to M_{i-1}$ such that $\operatorname{Ker} f_i = \operatorname{Im} f_{i+1}$. Then the sequence

$$\cdots \to M_{i+1} \xrightarrow{f_{i+1}} M_i \xrightarrow{f_i} M_{i-1} \to \cdots$$

is called an *exact sequence*. Equivalent definitions of R epimorphism, R monomorphism, and R isomorphism may be given by exact sequences. An R homomorphism $f: M \to T$ is an R epimorphism, R monomorphism, or R isomorphism according as

$$M \xrightarrow{f} T \to 0, \quad 0 \to M \xrightarrow{f} T, \quad \text{or } 0 \to M \xrightarrow{f} T \to 0$$

is exact, respectively, where 0 is the zero module. An exact sequence of the form

$$0 \to A \xrightarrow{f} B \xrightarrow{\pi} C \to 0$$

is called a *short exact sequence*. Note that A is isomorphic to $\operatorname{Im} f$, a submodule of B, and that C is isomorphic to $B/\operatorname{Im} f = B/\operatorname{Ker} \pi$.

DEFINITION. An exact sequence $M \xrightarrow{\mu} S \to 0$ is said to split if there is a map $S \xrightarrow{\rho} M$ such that $\mu\rho$ is identity on S. An exact sequence $0 \to S \xrightarrow{j} M$ *splits* if there is a map $M \xrightarrow{k} S$ such that kj is identity on S. The maps ρ and k are called *splitting homomorphisms*. An exact sequence that splits is called *split exact*.

If

$$M \xrightarrow{\mu} S \to 0$$

is split exact with splitting homomorphism ρ, then (since $S \cong \operatorname{Im} \rho$, where ρ is a monomorphism) if $x \in \operatorname{Im} \rho \cap \operatorname{Ker} \mu$, we should get $x = \rho(s)$ for some $s \in S$; hence, $0 = \mu(\rho(s)) = (\mu\rho)(s) = s$. So, $x = 0$. Also, if $m \in M$, then $\mu(m) \in S$, $(\rho\mu)(m) \in M$, and $m - (\rho\mu)(m) \in \operatorname{Ker} \mu$. That is, $M \cong \operatorname{Im} \rho \oplus \operatorname{Ker} \mu \cong S \oplus \operatorname{Ker} \mu$.

The reader may want to prove that if

$$0 \to S \overset{j}{\underset{k}{\rightleftarrows}} M$$

is split exact, then $M \cong \operatorname{Im} j \oplus \operatorname{Ker} k \cong S \oplus \operatorname{Ker} k \cong \operatorname{Im} k \oplus \operatorname{Ker} k$.

The short exact sequence $0 \to A \to B \to C \to 0$ is said to split if either end of it splits. In fact, if the short exact sequence splits at one end, it splits at the other end also. Moreover, $B = A \oplus C$. As an example of the first statement, suppose

$$0 \to A \xrightarrow{j} B \underset{\rho}{\overset{\pi}{\rightleftarrows}} C \to 0 \quad \text{exact,}$$

where ρ is a splitting homomorphism. We know that $B = \text{Im } \rho \oplus \text{Ker } \pi$, so $B = \text{Im } \rho \oplus \text{Im } j$. If $b \in B$, then $b = x + y$, $x \in \text{Im } \rho$, $y \in \text{Im } j$. Define $k: B \to A$ by $k(b) = j^{-1}(y)$. (Since $y \in \text{Im } j$ and j is a monomorphism, there is exactly one element $a \in A$ such that $j(a) = y$. We are denoting that element by $j^{-1}(y)$). The map k is the splitting homomorphism for $0 \to A \to B$. A similar argument shows that if the left end splits, then so does the right end. Since ρ and j are R monomorphisms, $B \cong A \oplus C$.

A useful fact concerning short exact sequences is the following: If A is an R submodule of B and

$$0 \to A \xrightarrow{j} B \to B/A \to 0 \tag{1.5}$$

is exact, where j is the injection of A into B, then expression (1.5) splits if and only if $A \ (\cong \text{Im } j)$ is a direct summand of B. For, if (1.5) splits, then from what we have just said, $B = A \oplus A/B$, so that A is a direct summand of B. Conversely, if $B \cong A \oplus C$, then a splitting homomorphism is the projection mapping of B onto A.

DEFINITION. An R module P is called a *projective R module* if diagram

$$\begin{array}{c} P \\ \downarrow \mu \\ A \xrightarrow{\pi} B \to 0 \quad \text{exact} \end{array}$$

can be embedded in the diagram

$$\begin{array}{c} P \\ {}^{\bar{\mu}}\swarrow \downarrow \mu \\ A \xrightarrow{\pi} B \to 0 \quad \text{exact} \end{array}$$

in such a way that $\pi\bar{\mu} = \mu$. The latter diagram is said to be commutative. Roughly speaking, P is projective if R homomorphisms of P can be lifted from factor modules (B) to modules (A).

DEFINITION. An R module F is called *free*, provided it has a *basis B;* that is, F is free, provided there is a subset B of F with the property that every $x \in F$ can be expressed uniquely in the form

$$x = \sum_{i=1}^{n} r_i b_i, \quad r_i \neq 0 \in R, \quad b_i \in B.$$

"Uniquely," here, means that $b_1 \cdots b_n$ are distinct elements of B, and if $x = \sum_1^m r_j' b_j'$ for distinct $b_1' \cdots b_m'$ and $r_j' \neq 0$, then each $b_j' = $ some b_i and $r_j' = r_i$.

An important property of free modules is that a free R module is projective: suppose the diagram

$$F$$
$$\downarrow \mu$$
$$A \xrightarrow{\pi} C \rightarrow 0 \quad \text{exact.}$$

We must exhibit an R homomorphism $\bar{\mu}: F \rightarrow A$. $\bar{\mu}$ is defined as follows:

For a basis element b, let $\bar{\mu}(b)$ be an element of the set $\{x \in A \,|\, \pi(x) = \mu(b)\}$; this is nonempty because π is an epimorphism. Now, for $x \in F$, form the unique representation $x = \sum r_i b_i$ and define $\bar{\mu}(x) = \sum r_i \bar{\mu}(b_i)$. Then one checks to see that $\bar{\mu}$ is an R homomorphism of F into A such that $\pi \bar{\mu} = \mu$ and, consequently, F is projective.

In the above construction of $\bar{\mu}$, we made use of another important property of free modules. If F is free with basis B and if g is any *function* from B to a module M, then g can be extended uniquely to a homomorphism of F to M. The process for extending g is the one used above to obtain $\bar{\mu}$, once $\bar{\mu}(b)$ had been defined for basis elements $b \in B$.

For any set T, we can construct a free module with a basis in one-to-one correspondence with T. Note first that R itself is a free module with a basis consisting of one element, the identity of R. To construct free modules with large bases, proceed as follows: Let T be a set and form $\oplus \sum R_t = \{g \,|\, g: T \rightarrow R\}$, with $g(t) = 0$ for all but a finite number of t. This is the direct sum of modules R_t, $t \in T$, where each R_t is R itself. Observe that $\oplus \sum R_t$ is free, with a basis T' consisting of functions g_t with the property that $g_t(t) = 1$ and $g_t(s) = 0$ for $s \neq t$. The basis T' is in one-to-one correspondence with the set T. The free module that we have just constructed will be called F_T, and we shall think of T as actually being the basis by identifying T with T' in F_T.

Theorem on Projectives. Let P be an R module. Then the following statements are equivalent:

(1) P is projective,
(2) Every exact sequence $M \rightarrow P \rightarrow 0$ splits, and
(3) P is a direct summand of a free R module F.

Proof

(a) $(1) \rightarrow (2)$. Consider the diagram

$$P$$
$$\downarrow i$$
$$M \underset{\pi}{\rightarrow} P \rightarrow 0 \quad \text{exact.}$$

Since P is projective, there is an R homomorphism $\mu\colon P \rightarrow M$ such that $\pi\mu = i$. That is, $M \rightarrow P \rightarrow 0$ splits.

(b) $(2) \rightarrow (3)$. There is a free R module F having as a basis the elements of P. Form the exact sequence

$$F \overset{\pi}{\rightarrow} P \rightarrow 0,$$

where π is the extension of $i\colon P \rightarrow P$. This sequence splits, and therefore $F = P \oplus \text{Ker } \pi$.

(c) $(3) \rightarrow (1)$. Consider

$$P$$
$$\downarrow \mu$$
$$A \overset{\pi}{\rightarrow} B \rightarrow 0.$$

By hypothesis, $F = P \oplus Q$ for some R module Q. Define $\mu'\colon F \rightarrow B$ by

$$\mu'(f) = \mu(x),$$

where $f = x + y, f \in F, x \in P, y \in Q$. Then μ' is an R homomorphism of the free R module F and may be lifted to an R homomorphism $\bar\mu'\colon F \rightarrow A$ such that $\pi\bar\mu' = \mu'$. Then the restriction μ_1 of $\bar\mu'$ to P has the property that $\pi\mu_1 = \mu$. This completes the proof of the theorem.

The following theorem shows that projectiveness goes over to direct summands and direct sums.

THEOREM. $\oplus \sum P_\alpha$ is projective if and only if each P_α is projective.

Proof. If each P_α is projective and we have the situation

$$\oplus \sum P_\alpha$$
$$\downarrow f$$
$$B \overset{\pi}{\rightarrow} A \rightarrow 0,$$

consider the restrictions $f_\alpha = f|_{P_\alpha}$ and lift each f_α to $\bar f_\alpha\colon P_\alpha \rightarrow B$ so that $\pi\bar f_\alpha = f_\alpha$. Let $\bar f = \sum \bar f_\alpha$ and it will do the job. Conversely, if $\oplus \sum P_\alpha$ is projective and we consider the diagram,

$$P_\beta$$
$$\downarrow f_\beta$$
$$B \rightarrow A \rightarrow 0.$$

Define $f: \oplus \sum P_\alpha \to A$ by $f = 0$ on P_α, $\alpha \neq \beta$, and $f = f_\beta$ on P_β. Lift f to $\bar{f}$ and restrict $\bar{f}$ back down to P_β. The restriction of $\bar{f}$ is the lifting of f_β.

DEFINITION. An R module Q is called *injective* if the diagram

$$0 \to A \xrightarrow{\pi} B \quad \text{exact}$$
$$\mu \downarrow$$
$$Q$$

can be embedded in the diagram

$$0 \to A \xrightarrow{\pi} B \quad \text{exact}$$
$$\mu \downarrow \swarrow \bar{\mu}$$
$$Q$$

in such a way that the latter diagram is commutative (that is, $\mu = \bar{\mu}\pi$).

Injectiveness is a concept "dual" to projectiveness (that is, all the arrows go the other way). At this point, we only mention it; later on, we shall investigate this concept.

It is probably wise to mention Zorn's lemma, which isn't a lemma at all. It is really an axiom concerning sets which is a valuable (and necessary) tool in many of the proofs we construct. First, we discuss some terminology.

A partially ordered set P has an order relation $\leq$ holding between some of its elements satisfying these rules:

(1) If $a \leq b$ and $b \leq c$, then $a \leq c$.
(2) If $a \leq b$ and $b \leq a$, then $a = b$.

A subset C of P is a chain in P if for any two elements a, b of C either $a \leq b$ or $b \leq a$. The chain C is bounded above in P if there exists $b \in P$ such that $c \leq b$ holds for all c in C.

Zorn's Lemma. If P is a partially ordered set with the property that every chain in P is bounded above, then there exists $m \in P$ with the property that if $m \leq x$, then $x = m$ (m is a maximal element of P).

We shall assume and use Zorn's lemma whenever it is convenient.

A finiteness condition, which we use in the next chapter, is "the minimum condition." A module M has minimum condition on submodules if every nonempty collection $\{M_\alpha\}$ of submodules has a minimal element. That is, there exists $M_0 \in \{M_\alpha\}$ such that there is no $M_\beta \in \{M_\alpha\}$ such that M_0 contains M_β properly. Minimum condition on left ideals means minimum condition on the ring considered as a left module over itself. Some rings have it (for example, fields, since they have so few left ideals) and some rings do not (the integers lack it).

Perhaps we should say something about the terms *homology* and *homological*. Strictly speaking, these terms refer to the *homology groups*, which are introduced in Chapter 3. However, it has become common practice to attach the term homological to almost anything connected with the homology groups. Following this practice, we shall apply the adjective "homological" to anything involving projectives, injectives, or splitting of exact sequences as well as to the homology groups themselves. Some people even go so far as to call homological "anything with little arrows in it."

(2)

Everybody Splits

The purpose of this chapter is to determine the structure of rings for which every module is projective. We shall show that this condition is equivalent to a number of other homological and ring theoretic concepts.

The motivation here is threefold. In the first place, we can think of the investigation as an example of a homological theory in which we raise a question about the structure of rings all of whose modules satisfy something homological. Such investigations are the latest algebraic rage.

In the second place, the homological concepts we need here are very simple. Thus, we can get results before the reader collapses under the burden of too much homological machinery (later chapters will show this to be a very real danger).

The third reason for launching our investigation is that we can give a very satisfying answer to the question we raise. The main part of the following structure theorem that we shall prove dates back to Wedderburn. It still remains one of the most powerful and frequently cited theorems in ring theory.

Structure Theorem for Semisimple Rings with Minimum Condition

The following six statements are equivalent:

(1) Every R module is projective.
(2) Every short exact sequence of R modules splits.
(3) Every R module is injective.
(4) Every nonzero R module is the direct sum of simple R submodules.
(5) R is the direct sum of a finite number of simple left ideals:

$$R = \oplus \sum_{i=1}^{n} L_i,$$

where each L_i is a simple left ideal and $L_i = Re_i$,
where $\{e_i\}_{i=1}^{n}$ is a set of orthogonal idempotents such that

$$\sum_{i=1}^{n} e_i = 1 \in R.$$

(6) $R = \oplus \sum_{j=1}^{r} R_j$, where R_j is a two-sided ideal and R_j is isomorphic as a ring to the complete ring of $n_j \times n_j$ matrices with entries in a division ring $\Delta_j, j = 1, 2, \cdots, r$.

Remarks. Any ring having the properties of the theorem is called a *semisimple ring with minimum condition on left ideals.* An examination of this theorem shows that we might just as well have stated the theorem for R right modules, the proof being essentially the same in either case. The important thing is that statement (6) does not involve either "rightness" or "leftness" of the modules. Thus statements (1) through (5), being equivalent to (6), which is in turn equivalent to (1) through (5) stated for R right modules, are equivalent to (1) through (5) stated for R right modules. Hence, all R modules are projective if and only if all R right modules are projective, and so on.

Proof of the Structure Theorem. The program is to prove $(1) \leftrightarrow (2) \leftrightarrow (3)$, $(2) \to (4)$, $(4) \to (5)$, $(5) \to (6)$, $(6) \to (5)$, and $(5) \to (2)$.

(a) $(1) \to (2)$. Assume all R modules are projective and examine the right end of a short exact sequence $A \xrightarrow{\mu} B \to 0$. Look at the diagram

$$
\begin{array}{ccc}
 & & B \\
 & \nearrow{\scriptstyle \nu} & \downarrow{\scriptstyle i} \\
A & \xrightarrow{\mu} B & \longrightarrow 0 \quad \text{exact,}
\end{array}
$$

and use the projectivity of B to get ν such that $\mu\nu = i$; that is, the splitting.

(b) $(2) \to (1)$. In the situation

$$
\begin{array}{c}
P \\
\downarrow{\scriptstyle f} \\
B \underset{\nu}{\overset{\pi}{\leftarrow\!\dashrightarrow}} A \to 0 \quad \text{exact,}
\end{array}
$$

splitting implies that π exists such that $\nu\pi = $ identity. Note that a lifting of f is πf; so, P is projective. The equivalence of (2) and (3) is analogous with all the arrows going the other way. Here we look at the left ends of short exact sequences.

(c) $(2) \to (3)$. Assume that all short exact sequences split. Let Q be any R module and let A and B be such that

$$
\begin{array}{c}
0 \longrightarrow A \underset{k}{\overset{j}{\underset{\dashleftarrow}{\longrightarrow}}} B \text{ is exact.} \\
\downarrow{\scriptstyle \mu} \\
Q
\end{array}
$$

There exists a splitting homomorphism $k: B \to A$ such that $kj = i$. Define $\bar{\mu}: B \to Q$ by $\bar{\mu} = \mu k$. Then $\bar{\mu} j = \mu kj = \mu$ and Q is injective.

(d) $(3) \to (2)$. Consider the diagram

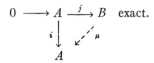

$$0 \longrightarrow A \xrightarrow{\ j\ } B \quad \text{exact.}$$

Since, by hypothesis, A is injective, there is $\mu: B \to A$ such that $\mu j = i$. Then μ is the splitting homomorphism of $0 \to A \to B$.

(e) $(2) \to (4)$. Let M be a nonzero R module. The first part of the proof is to show that M possesses simple R submodules. We use Zorn's lemma for this.

Let $x \in M$, $x \neq 0$, and consider the partially ordered (the ordering is set inclusion) family $\mathcal{P} = \{S | S \text{ is an } R \text{ submodule of } M, x \notin S\}$. Note that $0 \in \mathcal{P}$, so that $\mathcal{P}$ is nonempty. Let $\{S_\alpha\}_{\alpha \in \mathfrak{a}}$ be a chain in $\mathcal{P}$ and set

$$S_0 = \cup_{\alpha \in \mathfrak{a}} S_\alpha.$$

S_0 is an R submodule of M (since the S_α's form a chain) and $x \notin S_0$. Consequently, S_0 is an upper bound in $\mathcal{P}$ for the chain $\{S_\alpha\}_{\alpha \in \mathfrak{a}}$, and by Zorn's lemma, $\mathcal{P}$ has a maximal element S.

Since $0 \to S \to M \to M/S \to 0$ splits, S is a direct summand of M (say, $M = S \oplus T$ for some T). Now we claim that T is a simple R submodule of M. For, suppose T is not a simple R submodule of M, then there exists U an R submodule of M such that $T \supset U \supset (0)$. Again, since $0 \to U \to T \to T/U \to 0$ splits, we may write $T = U \oplus V$ for some R submodule V of M. The R submodule V is nonzero, since $V = T/U$ and $U \subset T$. Hence, $M = S \oplus U \oplus V$. Now $x \in M$, $x \notin S$ implies that $x = s + u = s' + v$, where $s \in S$, $s' \in S$, $u \in U$, and $v \in V$. This is because S is maximal with regard to not containing x, and so $S \oplus U$ and $S \oplus V$ must both contain x. But $0 = (s - s') + u - v$ gives $u = 0$ whence $x = s \in S$, which is contrary to the choice of S. That is, T is simple.

Another application of Zorn's lemma completes the proof.

Let $\mathcal{S}$ be the collection of all independent families of simple R submodules of M. Our first use of Zorn's lemma shows $\mathcal{S}$ is nonempty; a simple submodule all by itself is independent. The collection $\mathcal{S}$ is partially ordered by inclusion. Note that the elements of $\mathcal{S}$ are sets of independent, simple modules. Let $\{T_\alpha\}_{\alpha \in \mathfrak{B}}$ be a chain in $\mathcal{S}$ and let C be the union of the families T_α. C is an upper bound for the chain $\{T_\alpha\}_{\alpha \in \mathfrak{B}}$, and all we have to do to apply Zorn's lemma is to show that $C \in \mathcal{S}$. Let S_0 be a simple R submodule in C, and let $\sum$ be the sum of all the other R submodules in C. Suppose $S_0 \cap \sum \neq (0)$. Since S_0 is simple, $S_0 \subseteq \sum$. Let $x \in S_0$, $x \neq 0$, and write $x = x_1 + x_2 + \cdots + x_m$, where $x_i \in S_i$, $S_i \neq S_0$, $i = 1, 2, \cdots, m$.

Now C is the union of a chain and $S_0, S_1, \cdots, S_m$ are in C, so there is $\alpha \in \mathfrak{B}$ such that T_α contains $S_0, S_1, \cdots, S_m$. But T_α is an independent family whence $x_1 + x_2 + \cdots + x_m - x = 0$ means that $x = 0$. The contradiction implies that $S_0 \cap \Sigma = (0)$ and $C \in \mathcal{S}$. Zorn's lemma now tells us that $\mathcal{S}$ contains a maximal element $U = \{S_\gamma\}_{\gamma \in \mathcal{D}}$. Let $N = \sum_{\gamma \in \mathcal{D}} S_\gamma$. N is an R submodule of M and therefore is a direct summand of M, $M = N \oplus T$. If $T \neq (0)$, then T contains a simple R submodule of M independent of N, which is contrary to the choice of U. Therefore, $T = (0)$ and $M = N = \oplus \sum_{\gamma \in \mathcal{D}} S_\gamma$.

(f) $(4) \rightarrow (5)$. Since the R submodules of R are the left ideals of R, (4) implies that $R = \oplus \sum_{\alpha \in \mathcal{Q}} L_\alpha$, where the L_α are simple left ideals in R. The index set $\mathcal{Q}$ is actually finite. To show this, we must make use of the standing hypothesis that $1 \in R$. Let $1 \in R$ be written $1 = e_{\alpha_1} + e_{\alpha_2} + \cdots + e_{\alpha_n}$, $e_{\alpha_i} \in L_{\alpha_i}$, $i = 1, 2, \cdots, n$; and let L_α be different from any of $L_{\alpha_1}, \cdots, L_{\alpha_n}$. Pick $x \in L_\alpha$. Then

$$x = x1 = xe_{\alpha_1} + xe_{\alpha_2} + \cdots + xe_{\alpha_n} \in \sum_{i=1}^{n} L_{\alpha_i}.$$

Since L_α is independent of $L_{\alpha_1}, \cdots, L_{\alpha_n}$, x must be zero. Hence, $L_\alpha = (0)$ and $\mathcal{Q}$ is finite.

Write

$$R = \oplus \sum_{i=1}^{n} L_i,$$

where

$$1 = e_1 + e_2 + \cdots + e_n, \quad e_i \in L_i, \quad i = 1, 2, \cdots, n.$$

Since $0 = e_i - e_i = e_i1 - e_i = e_ie_1 + e_ie_2 + \cdots + e_ie_{i-1} + (e_i^2 - e_i) + e_ie_{i+1} + \cdots + e_ie_n$, the independence of the L_i's gives $e_i^2 = e_i$ and $e_ie_j = 0$ if $j \neq i$. This holds for $i = 1, 2, \cdots, n$, and therefore the elements $e_1, \cdots, e_n$ form an orthogonal set of idempotents in R. Finally, $0 \neq e_i^2 \in Re_i \subseteq L_i$, and since L_i is simple, $Re_i = L_i$, $i = 1, 2, \cdots, n$.

(g) $(5) \rightarrow (6)$. R is a direct sum of finitely many simple left ideals:

$$R = \sum_{i=1}^{n} L_i.$$

Now group together those L_i that are isomorphic as R modules. Let R_1 be the direct sum of all those L_i that are isomorphic to L_1; let R_2 be the direct sum of the next set of isomorphic simple modules, and so on. We continue in this manner until we have

$$R = \oplus \sum_{j=1}^{r} R_j,$$

where each R_j is the direct sum of isomorphic left ideals L_i, and for $j \neq k$, the summands of R_j are not isomorphic to any of those in R_k. At the moment we know that the R_j are left ideals; in the following discussion, we shall show that they are actually two-sided ideals.

We shall show that for $j \neq k$, $R_j R_k = 0$. Each element of R_j is a sum of elements from the simple summands of R_j; and similarly for R_k. It is therefore sufficient if we show that $L_i L = 0$, where L_i is any summand of R_j and L is any summand of R_k. But if $L_i L \neq 0$, there is an element $z \in L$ such that $L_i z \neq 0$, and this allows us to define:

$$\phi L_i \to L \quad \text{by} \quad \phi(x) = xz.$$

One checks to see that ϕ is a nonzero homomorphism of L_i to L, and it is therefore an isomorphism, since both L_i and L are simple. But this contradicts the construction of R_j and R_k. Thus, we conclude that $R_j R_k = 0$ and that each R_j is a two-sided ideal.

To prove the last part of statement (6), it suffices to let

$$R = \oplus \sum_{i=1}^{n} L_i$$

with

$$L_1 \cong L_2 \cong \cdots L_n$$

and prove that R is isomorphic as a ring to the complete ring of $n \times n$ matrices with entries from a division ring Δ.

By Schur's lemma, the ring Δ of all R homomorphisms of L_1 into itself is a division ring. It is from this Δ that the entries for our matrices will be taken. What we need to do is to characterize these R homomorphisms in some convenient way. We do this as follows: Let f be an R homomorphism from L_i into L_j. Now $f(e_i) \in Re_j$ (say, $f(e_i) = re_j$) for some $r \in R$. Then $f(e_i) = f(e_i^2) = e_i f(e_i) = e_i re_j$. Since for $x \in L_i$, $x = xe_i$ (because $x = ye_i$ for some $y \in R$ and $xe_i = ye_i^2 = ye_i = x$), we get $f(x) = f(xe_i) = xe_i re_j$. That is, f acts on the elements of L_i as right multiplication by $e_i re_j$, where $f(e_i) = e_i re_j$. It follows that the additive group of all R homomorphisms of L_i into L_j is group-isomorphic to $e_i Re_j$.

Now suppose that we have two homomorphisms, f from L_i to L_j and g from L_j to L_k. If f is caused by a right multiplication by the element $e_i re_j$ and g is a right multiplication by $e_j se_k$, then the composition gf is given by a right multiplication by $e_i re_j se_k$. Note that the elements causing the homomorphisms multiply in the order opposite to the way we usually compose the homomorphisms f and g.

We now identify the homomorphisms with the elements that cause them. When we compose the homomorphisms, we multiply the elements, and when we add the homomorphisms, we add the elements. We work with the elements so that xy means "first the homomorphism caused by x, then the one caused by y." Choose $g_i \in e_i R e_i$ to be a fixed R isomorphism of L_1 onto L_i for each i. We denote by g_i^{-1} the element in $e_i R e_1$ that gives the inverse of g_i. These elements satisfy the following conditions:

$$g_i^{-1} g_i = e_i, \quad g_i^{-1} g = e_1.$$

Now let r be an element of R and consider the element $g_i e_i r e_j g_j^{-1}$. This element represents the composition of three homomorphisms: first, g_i from L_1 to L_i; then $e_i r e_j$ from L_i to L_j; and finally g_j^{-1} from L_j back to L_1. Thus, the element $g_i e_i r e_j g_j^{-1}$ is an element of our division ring Δ.

For an element r of R, define the matrix $M(r)$ to have $g_i e_i r e_j g_j^{-1}$ in the i, j position. The entries in these matrices come from the division ring Δ. In the following discussion, we shall show that the correspondence $r \to M(r)$ is a ring isomorphism between R and the complete ring of $n \times n$ matrices over Δ. In addition to using the properties of the g_i's developed above, the proof uses the fact that the elements e_i are orthogonal idempotents whose sum is the identity of R. Note that this is part of the assumption (5) of the theorem.

(h) $r \to M(r)$ is additive. Let

$$r_1 \to M(r_1) = (g_i e_i r_1 e_j g_j^{-1})$$

and

$$r_2 \to M(r_2) = (g_i e_i r_2 e_j g_j^{-1}).$$

Then

$$M(r_1) + M(r_2) = (g_i e_i r_1 e_j g_j^{-1} + g_i e_i r_2 e_j g_j^{-1})$$
$$= (g_i e_i (r_1 + r_2) e_j g_j^{-1})$$
$$= M(r_1 + r_2).$$

(i) $r \to M(r)$ is multiplicative. Let $r_1 \to M(r_1)$ and $r_2 \to M(r_2)$. The (i, j) entry of $M(r_1) M(r_2)$ is

$$\sum_{k=1}^{n} (g_i e_i r_1 e_k g_k^{-1})(g_k e_k r_2 e_j g_j^{-1}) = \sum_{k=1}^{n} g_i e_i r_1 e_k r_2 e_j g_j^{-1}$$
$$= g_i e_i r_1 \left(\sum_{k=1}^{n} e_k \right) r_2 e_j g_j^{-1}$$
$$= g_i e_i (r_1 r_2) e_j g_j^{-1},$$

which is the (i, j) entry of $M(r_1 r_2)$.

(j) $r \to M(r)$ is one to one. Ler $r \in R$, $r \neq 0$. If, for every pair e_i, e_j it were true that $e_i r e_j = 0$, then we would have

$$0 = \sum_{i,j=1}^{n} e_i r e_j$$

$$= \sum_{j=1}^{n} \left(\sum_{i=1}^{n} e_i r e_j \right)$$

$$= \sum_{j=1}^{n} 1 r e_j = 1r \sum_{j=1}^{n} e_j$$

$$= 1r1 = r \neq 0.$$

Hence, there is some pair e_i, e_j such that $e_i r e_j \neq 0$. Then $e_i r e_j$ is a nonzero R homomorphism of L_i into L_j. Since L_i is simple, $e_i r e_j$ is an R isomorphism, whence $g_i e_i r e_j g_j^{-1}$ gives an R isomorphism, and hence is a nonzero element of Δ. Thus $M(r) \neq 0$.

(k) $r \rightarrow M(r)$ is onto. It suffices to show that if i, j is a pair of indices and if $\delta \in \Delta$, then there is some $r \in R$ such that $M(r)$ has all entries zero except the (i, j) entry, which is δ. Now $g_i^{-1} \delta g_j : L_i \rightarrow L_j$. Therefore, there exists an element $e_i r e_j \in e_i R e_j$ such that $e_i r e_j = g_i^{-1} \delta g_j$. That is, $\delta = g_i e_i r e_j g_j^{-1}$ and so the (i, j) entry of $M(e_i r e_j)$ is δ. All other entries of $M(e_i r e_j)$ are zero, since the (l, k) entry $(l \neq i$ or $k \neq j)$ is $g_l e_i r e_j g_k$, which is of the form

$$(e_l r_l e_i)(e_i r e_j)(e_k r_k e_l),$$

for some r_l, $r_k \in R$, which is zero unless both $l = i$ and $k = j$.

(l) $(6) \rightarrow (5)$. R is the ring direct sum of finitely many complete matrix rings. It therefore suffices to show that the complete $n \times n$ matrix ring Δ_n is a finite direct sum of simple left ideals, each of which is generated over Δ_n by an idempotent matrix such that these idempotents are orthogonal and their sum is the identity matrix.

Let L_i be the set of all $n \times n$ matrices having zeros in all entries not lying in the ith column and having arbitrary elements from Δ in the ith column. It can easily be checked that L_i is a minimal left ideal (and hence simple). Moreover, L_i is generated over Δ_n by the matrix K_i having all entries zero except the (i, i) entry, which is 1. Consequently,

$$\Delta_n = L_1 \oplus L_2 \cdots \oplus L_n = \Delta_n K_1 \oplus \Delta_n K_2 \oplus \cdots \oplus \Delta_n K_n,$$

where the K_i's are orthogonal idempotents whose sum is the identity matrix. This proves statement (5).

(m) $(5) \rightarrow (2)$. Let

$$R = \oplus \sum_{i=1}^{n} L_i,$$

L_i, a simple left ideal. Let M be an R module and let N be an R submodule of M. We shall show that N is a direct summand of M, and this implies that every short exact sequence of R modules splits.

Using a Zorn's lemma argument, it is always possible to find an R submodule T of M maximal with respect to the property $N \cap T = (0)$. The proof of this is left to the reader. Now $M \supseteq N \oplus T$. Suppose there exists $x \in M, x \notin N \oplus T$.

There is an index i such that $L_i x \not\subseteq N \oplus T$; for, if $L_i x \subseteq N \oplus T$ for each i, then

$$x \in Rx = \sum_{i=1}^{n} L_i x \subseteq N \oplus T,$$

contrary to the choice of x. So, for some i, $L_i x \not\subseteq N \oplus T$ (and, in particular, $L_i x \neq (0)$), the mapping $L_i \to M$ defined by $l \to lx$ is an R homomorphism of the R module L_i onto the R submodule $L_i x$ of M. Since L_i has no proper nonzero left ideals, and since $L_i x \neq (0)$, it follows that $L_i \cong L_i x$, and so $L_i x$ is simple. But then $L_i x \cap N \oplus T = (0)$ and $(L_i x \oplus T) \cap N = (0)$, contrary to the choice of T. Hence, $M = N \oplus T$, N is a direct summand of M and statement (2) has been proven.

This completes the proof of the theorem. One of the important aspects of this theorem is that it reduces the structure problems for semisimple rings, with minimum condition to the structure problems for division rings. The latter problems have been extensively investigated, but we shall not discuss them here.

In the statement of the structure theorem there were some direct sum decompositions, conditions (5) and (6). Whenever one sees such a decomposition, it is normal to ask about the degree to which the decomposition is unique.

We shall show that the decomposition (5) is "unique up to isomorphism." By this we mean that if

$$\oplus \sum_{}^{n} L_i = R = \oplus \sum_{}^{m} L_j'$$

are two decompositions of the type (5), then $n = m$ and there is a one-to-one correspondence between the L_i and the L_j' such that the corresponding left ideals are isomorphic. In the following theorem, we shall prove a slight generalization of this fact.

First Uniqueness Theorem.   If M is an R module and

$$\oplus \sum_{}^{n} S_i = M = \oplus \sum_{}^{m} S_j'$$

are two direct sum decompositions of M with simple summands S_i and S_j', then $n = m$ and there is a one-to-one correspondence between the S_i and S_j', with corresponding modules isomorphic.

Proof. We induce on n the smaller of m and n. For $n = 1$, M is itself simple and $m = 1$, for otherwise M would have nonzero proper submodules.

Now suppose that the theorem has been established for integers less than n. Suppose also that

$$\oplus \sum_{i=1}^{n} S_i = M = \oplus \sum_{j=1}^{m} S_j'$$

and that the S_i, S_j' are simple. There exists an index k such that $\pi_k'(S_1) \neq 0$, where π_k' is a projection on S_k'; for, if $\pi_k'(S_1) = 0$ for all k, that would imply that $S_1 = 0$. Since both S_1 and S_k' are simple, we see that π_k' restricted to S_1 gives an isomorphism of S_1 onto S_k'. Note that this implies $(\text{Ker } \pi_k') \cap S_1 = 0$.

We now show that $S_2 \oplus \cdots \oplus S_n \cong S_1' \oplus \cdots S_{k-1}' \oplus S_{k+1}' \cdots \oplus S_m'$. This will be sufficient, since the induction hypothesis would then imply that $n = m$ and the S_i $(i \geq 2)$ are in one-to-one correspondence with the $S_j'(j \neq k)$ with corresponding modules isomorphic.

First we have $S_1 \cap [S_1' \oplus \cdots \oplus S_{k-1}' \oplus S_{k+1}' \oplus \cdots \oplus S_m'] = 0$ because the term in brackets is $\text{Ker } \pi_k'$. This, in turn, implies that $T = S_1 + [S_1' \oplus \cdots \oplus S_{k-1}' \oplus S_{k+1}' \oplus \cdots \oplus S_m']$ properly contains $S_1' \oplus \cdots \oplus S_{k-1}' \oplus S_{k+1}' \oplus \cdots \oplus S_m'$. Consequently, T must contain a nonzero element of S_k', and therefore all of S_k'. Thus, we see that $T = M$. It follows that the sum

$$S_1 \oplus [S_1' \oplus \cdots \oplus S_{k-1}' \oplus S_k' \oplus \cdots \oplus S_m'] = M$$

is actually direct and $S_1' \oplus \cdots \oplus S_{k-1}' \oplus S_{k+1}' \oplus \cdots \oplus S_m'$ and $S_2 \oplus \cdots \oplus S_n$ are isomorphic to each other, since both are isomorphic to M/S_1. This completes the proof of the uniqueness theorem.

Perhaps this is a good place to check a point that we mentioned briefly a few pages back when discussing the structure theorem. We said that the rings satisfying the structure theorem were called semisimple rings with minimum condition. However, at that time, we did not show that these rings do in fact have minimum condition on left ideals (and hence on right ideals as well by the left right symmetry of the structure theorem).

The term "theorem" applied to this is not appropriate ("If R is a semisimple ring with minimum condition on left ideals, then R has minimum condition on left ideals."), so let us call it a remark.

Remark. If R satisfies the conditions of the structure theorem, then R has minimum conditions on left ideals (and also on right ideals).

Let $\{L_\alpha\}$ be a nonempty collection of left ideals in R. Each L_α is a direct summand of R and is the direct sum of simple modules. Each L_α is actually the direct sum of a finite number of simple modules; for, otherwise, the ring itself would be the direct sum of an infinite number of simple modules, a situation that is ruled out because R possesses an identity.

Now let $L_{\alpha_0} \in \{L_\alpha\}$ be selected so that it has the fewest number of summands when represented as a direct sum of simple modules. By the uniqueness theorem, this number is the same no matter how L_α is represented as a direct sum of simple modules. If L is properly contained in L_{α_0}, then $L_{\alpha_0} = L \oplus C$ (every submodule is a direct summand), and the number of simple summands in L is less than the number for L_{α_0}. Thus, our method for choosing L_{α_0} does give rise to a minimal element of $\{L_\alpha\}$.

Let us now return to the uniqueness problems associated with the direct sum decomposition in the structure theorem.

In the following discussion, we shall show that the decomposition (6) is even "more unique" than (5). First we give a lemma that, together with condition (6), helps to explain the origin of the term "semisimple."

Lemma. If R is the ring of all $m \times m$ matrices with coefficients in a division ring Δ, then R is a simple ring (R has exactly two two-sided ideals).

Proof. Let $A = (a_{ij})$ be a nonzero matrix in R. We shall show that the two-sided ideal containing A must contain a unit of the ring R and must therefore be all of R.

Let $E_{s,t}$ be the matrix with $1 \in \Delta$ in the (s, t) position and 0 in all other positions. Suppose that our matrix A has an entry $d \neq 0$ in the (i, j) position. Now form the element $E_{ki}AE_{jk}$ and check to see that this matrix has d in the kk position and zero everywhere else. Form the element

$$X = \sum_{k=1}^{m} E_{ki}AE_{jk}$$

and note that X has d repeated down the diagonal and zero off the diagonal. But the matrix X has an inverse X^{-1}, the diagonal matrix with d^{-1} down the diagonal. Thus, any ideal containing $A \neq 0$ must contain the identity and must be the whole ring.

Note that the preceding lemma shows that the decomposition (6) of the structure theorem is a decomposition into the direct sum of *simple* ideals. In the following discussion, we shall prove that such a decomposition is unique.

Second Uniqueness Theorem. If

$$R = \oplus \sum_{i=1}^{n} R_i \quad \text{and} \quad R = \oplus \sum_{j=1}^{m} R_j'$$

are two ring direct sum decompositions, where each R_i and R_j' is a simple ring with identity, then $n = m$ and each R_i is some R_j'.

Proof. Note the strength of the conclusion: Each R_i *is* some R_j'; this is stronger than "is isomorphic to."

The hypothesis implies that R has an identity; so, for each i, $R_iR = R_i$. Apply this to the equation $R = \oplus \sum_{j=1}^{m} R_j'$ and obtain $R_i = \sum_{j=1}^{m} R_iR_j'$. Each

$R_i R_j'$ is a two-sided ideal of R_i and so must be either R_i or zero. All cannot be zeros, so there exists R_j' such that $R_i = R_i R_j'$. Two such R_j' do not exist, for if $R_i R_k' = R_i = R_i R_j'$, then both R_j' and R_k' contain the ideal R_i. Now examine the equation $R_i = R_i R_j'$ and note that this is a two-sided ideal of R_j' and must therefore equal R_j'. Thus, we see that $R_i = R_j'$.

COROLLARY. If R is a semisimple ring with minimum condition, then R has the same number of nonisomorphic, simple, left modules as it has nonisomorphic, simple, right modules.

Proof. Let S be a simple R module where R is a semisimple ring with minimum condition. By the structure theorem,

$$R = \oplus \sum_1^n Re_i,$$

where each Re_i is a simple, left ideal of R. There must exist e_i among the idempotents and $s \in S$ such that $e_i s \neq 0$; for, otherwise, $RS = 0$. Now we can define $\phi: Re_i \to S$ by $\phi(xe_i) = xe_i s$, and we observe that this is a nonzero homomorphism of Re_i to S. Since both Re_i and S are simple, this must actually be an isomorphism. Thus, every simple R module is isomorphic to one of the simple, left ideal, direct summands of R.

In the proof of $(5) \to (6)$ in the structure theorem, the two-sided ideal R_j was constructed by grouping together those simple left ideals L_i that were isomorphic. Hence, there are the same number of simple, nonisomorphic, left modules as there are simple two-sided ideals R_i in the decomposition (6).

But the decomposition (6) is unique and two-sided; hence, the same proof with left replaced by right shows that there are the same number of simple right modules as there are two-sided ideals in the decomposition (6). This completes the proof of the corollary.

We shall make use of the above corollary in the problems at the end of this chapter and again in Chapter 5.

The hypothesis of the next theorem is often taken to be the definition of semisimple rings with minimum condition. For this theorem, we shall momentarily drop our assumption that all our rings have identities. Note that in the process of proving the theorem, we shall show that the ring does have an identity.

DEFINITION. A left ideal L is said to be *nilpotent* if there is a positive integer n such that $L^n = (0)$, where $L^n = L^{n-1}(L)$. Equivalently, L is nilpotent if for some n the product of any n elements of L is zero.

THEOREM. If R is a ring with minimum condition on left ideals and has no nonzero nilpotent left ideals, then R is a semisimple ring with minimum condition.

Proof. We must first show that R can be written as a sum of simple left ideals, each of which is idempotent-generated. We begin by breaking off one simple left ideal.

Since the minimum condition holds, a simple left ideal L may be found (minimal among the set of nonzero left ideals). $L^2 \neq (0)$ and so $L^2 = L$. There is an $x \in L$ such that $Lx \neq (0)$, simplicity of L implying that $Lx = L$. Also, there is $e \in L$, $e \neq 0$, such that $ex = x$. Right multiplication by x is an R isomorphism of L onto Lx (since L is simple); hence, $(e^2 - e)x = 0$ implies that $e^2 = e$. Since $0 \neq e^2 \in Re \subseteq L$ implies that $Re = L$, Re is a simple, idempotent-generated, left ideal. Moreover, $R = Re \oplus L_1$ and $L_1e = (0)$, where $L_1 = \{y - ye | y \in R\}$.

Now assume that

$$R = Re_1 \oplus Re_2 \oplus \cdots \oplus Re_n \oplus L_n,$$

where each Re_i is a simple left ideal and $e_1, e_2, \cdots, e_n$ are orthogonal idempotents such that $L_ne_i = (0)$ for each i. We shall prove that either $L_n = (0)$ or that there is $e_{n+1} \in L_n$ such that $L_n = Re_{n+1} \oplus L_{n+1}$, where Re_{n+1} is a simple left ideal in R such that e_{n+1} is an idempotent orthogonal to e_1, e_2, $\cdots$, e_n and $L_{n+1}e_{n+1} = (0)$. For, suppose $L_n \neq (0)$. By the preceding argument, there is an idempotent $e' \in L_n$ such that $L_n = Re' \oplus L_{n+1}$, where Re' is a simple left ideal and $L_{n+1}e' = (0)$. Clearly, $e'e_i = 0$ for $i = 1, 2, \cdots, n$. Now it need not be true that $e_ie' = 0$, so we pick another idempotent $e_{n+1} = e' - ee'$, where $e = e_1 + e_2 + \cdots + e_n$, which has the required properties. That is (and these are easily verified), e_{n+1} is a nonzero idempotent that is orthogonal to each $e_j, j = 1, 2, \cdots, n$, and $L_{n+1}e_{n+1} = (0)$. Since $Re_{n+1} \subseteq Re'$, $Re_{n+1} = Re'$ and Re_{n+1} is a simple left ideal. The minimum condition implies that for some $n + 1$, $L_{n+1} = (0)$; for, otherwise, the collection $\{L_n\}$ would not contain a minimal element. Thus, $R = Re_1 \oplus Re_2 \oplus \cdots \oplus Re_n$.

It remains only to show that R has an identity 1. Let $1 = e_1 + e_2 + \cdots + e_n$. Then 1 is a right identity for R, since for $r = r_1e_1 + r_2e_2 + \cdots + r_ne_n \in R$,

$$(r_1e_1 + \cdots + r_ne_n)(e_1 + \cdots + e_n) = r_1e^2 + \cdots + r_ne_n^2$$
$$= r_1e_1 + \cdots + r_ne_n = r.$$

For any two elements $y, r \in R$, we have the following equation:

$$y(1r - r) = y1(1r - r) = y(1^2r - 1r) = 0.$$

Thus, for fixed r, the additive group $\{1r - r\}$ generated by $1r - r$ is a left ideal. If $\{1r - r\}$ is not (0), then $\{1r - r\}^2 = (0)$, contrary to hypothesis; so, $1r = r$. Consequently, 1 is the identity for R. This completes the proof.

COROLLARY. A ring R with minimum condition on left ideals is semisimple if and only if R has no nontrivial, nilpotent, left ideals.

Proof. If R is semisimple, every left ideal L_1 is a direct summand by (2) of the main theorem, $R = L_1 \oplus L_2$. Let $1 = e_1 + e_2$ and check to see that e_1 is an idempotent in L_1 and that $L_1 = Re_1$. Thus, every nonzero left ideal contains an idempotent and therefore cannot be nilpotent.

EXERCISES

Let G be a finite group of order n and let K be a field. Define the group algebra $A = K(G)$ to be the set of all functions from G to K, where the functions are added image-wise in K. Define the product of two functions by the convolution formula:

$$h * f(g) = \sum_{\alpha \epsilon G} h(g\alpha^{-1})f(\alpha).$$

Another way to think of the group algebra is to let A be a K vector space with a basis consisting of the elements of G. Multiply basis elements by the group multiplication and extend this multiplication linearly to all vector space.

1. Prove that these two definitions give rise to the same algebra (that is, find a natural isomorphism).

   Now let M be an A module with an A submodule T. Notice that these are also K modules and that the exact sequence

$$0 \to T \to M \xrightarrow{\pi} M/T \to 0$$

   can be thought of either as a sequence of K modules or as a sequence of A modules.

2. Show that the above sequence splits as a K sequence.

   Let β be the splitting that is $\pi\beta = $ identity on M/T. Alas, β need not be an A homomorphism, but if it were, we should have a splitting of the sequence as an exact sequence of A modules. However, sometimes we can manufacture such a splitting out of β.

   Form the mapping $g^{-1}\beta g$ from M/T to M. (This means: "first operate by g in M/T, follow by β, and then operate by g^{-1} in M.")

3. Now define

$$\beta' = \sum_{g \epsilon G} g^{-1}\beta g$$

   and check to see how close it is to being a splitting of A modules.

4. Prove this. If the characteristic of K does not divide the order of G, then A is a semisimple ring with minimum condition.

5. Prove the converse of the preceding theorem by examining the ideal in A generated by the element $\sum_{g \in G} g$ in the case the characteristic does divide the order of G.

6. Let us prove the following theorem:

   THEOREM. In a ring with minimum condition on left ideals, if L is a nonnilpotent left ideal, then there is an element y in L such that $y^n \neq 0$ for all n.

   Proof. (a) Find $L' \subseteq L$ such that $0 \neq L'^2 = L'$. Why does this exist?
   (b) Now choose $M \subseteq L'$ minimal with respect to the properties $L'M \neq 0$, $M \subseteq L'$. Can this be done?
   (c) Show that there exists x in M such that $L'x = M$.
   (d) Now show that there exists y in $L' \subseteq L$ such that $yx = x$, and determine whether this y will do the job. This completes the proof of the theorem.

7. Prove that in a ring with minimum condition on left ideals, a left ideal is nilpotent if and only if every element in it is nilpotent. (A nilpotent element is one that gives zero when raised to some power.)

8. Prove that in a ring with minimum condition on left ideals, there exist maximal nilpotent left ideals ("maximal among the set of nilpotent left ideals").

9. Prove (in any ring) that the sum of two nilpotent left ideals is again nilpotent.

10. Show that in any ring with minimum condition, there is a unique maximal nilpotent left ideal N containing all nilpotent left ideals.

11. Prove that if L is a nilpotent left ideal, then so is Lx for any x in R.

12. Show that the left ideal N of Exercise 10 is actually two-sided.

13. Prove that if R has minimum condition on left ideals, then R/N is a semisimple ring with minimum condition on left ideals.

14. Consider N^i/N^{i+1} as a left R/N module (is this OK?), and determine why it is the direct sum of a finite number of simple submodules.

15. Prove: If R has minimum condition on left ideals, then R has a composition series of left ideals. (That is, a finite chain of left ideals $R = L_0 \supset L_1 \supset \cdots \supset L_n = (0)$ such that each L_i/L_{i+1} is simple.)

Note. The ideal N defined in Exercise 10 is called the *radical* of R. We shall refer to it again.

16. Prove that a ring with minimum condition on left ideals has the same number of nonisomorphic, simple, left modules as nonisomorphic, simple, right modules. The idea is to show that simple R modules are simple R/N modules, and conversely.

17. Let R be the ring of $n \times n$ matrices with coefficients in a field K having zero in every entry above the diagonal. Find the radical of R and prove that R/N is commutative.

(3)

Complexes, Homology, and Ext

In this chapter we plan to define Ext and establish a few of its basic properties. As the reader will note, the process takes a considerable amount of space and lots of machinery, some of which will be used in later chapters.

DEFINITION. A *complex* (sometimes called a *graded differential complex*) is a sequence of R modules

$$C = \{C_n\}_{n=-\infty}^{\infty}$$

together with a collection of R homomorphisms

$$\{d_n: C_n \to C_{n-1}\}_{n=-\infty}^{\infty}$$

or

$$\{d_n: C_n \to C_{n+1}\}_{n=-\infty}^{\infty}$$

called *differentials* such that

$$d_{n-1}d_n = 0 \quad \text{or} \quad d_{n+1}d_n = 0.$$

For simplicity in the following discussion, we shall treat only the case that the differential goes down ($d_n: C_n \to C_{n-1}$). All the analogous properties can be shown in the other case by merely renumbering. In application, both cases will occur.

If C is a complex of R modules with differentials $d_n: C_n \to C_{n-1}$, then Ker $d_n \supseteq$ Im d_{n+1}. Let $H_n(C) =$ Ker $d_n/$Im d_{n+1}. The groups, $H_n(C)$, are called the *homology groups* of the complex. If $H_n(C) = (0)$ for every n, then the complex is an exact sequence, and conversely.

If A and C are two complexes of R modules with differentials $d_n^A: A_n \to A_{n-1}$ and $d_n^C: C_n \to C_{n-1}$, respectively, then a *complex map* $f: A \to C$ is a collection of R homomorphisms $f_n: A_n \to C_n$ such that the following diagram is commutative:

$$
\begin{array}{ccc}
\cdots \to A_n & \xrightarrow{d_n^A} & A_{n-1} \to \cdots \\
\downarrow{f_n} & & \downarrow{f_{n-1}} \\
\cdots \to C_n & \xrightarrow{d_n^C} & C_{n-1} \to \cdots
\end{array}
$$

That is, for each n, $f_{n-1}d_n^A = d_n^C f_n$.

27

In the following text, we are going to drop the subscripts and super-scripts on differentials and complex maps except in those cases where confusion would otherwise result. Usually it will be clear from the context which sub-scripts and superscripts are called for.

Proposition. If A and C are complexes of R modules, then a complex map $f: A \rightarrow C$ induces (for each n) an R homomorphism $f_*: H_n(A) \rightarrow H_n(C)$.

Proof. Consider $f_n: A_n \rightarrow C_n$. Notice that the relation $f_n d_{n+1} = d_{n+1} f_{n+1}$ implies that $f_n(\operatorname{Im} d_{n+1}) \subseteq \operatorname{Im} d_{n+1}$ in C_n. Thus, f_n induces $f'_n: A_n/\operatorname{Im} d_{n+1} \rightarrow C_n/\operatorname{Im} d_{n+1}$. Similarly, the relation $d_n f_n = f_{n-1} d_n$ shows that $f_n(\operatorname{Ker} d_n) \subseteq \operatorname{Ker} d_n$ in C_n. That is, we have the induced map

$$f'_n|_{H_n(A)}: H_n(A) \rightarrow H_n(C).$$

This mapping is f_*.

DEFINITION. The sequence

$$0 \rightarrow A \xrightarrow{j} B \xrightarrow{\pi} C \rightarrow 0$$

where A, B, C, and 0 are complexes of R modules (0 is the complex of zero R modules). The sequence is called an *exact sequence of complexes* if $0 \rightarrow A$, j, π, and $C \rightarrow 0$ are complex maps and

$$0 \rightarrow A_n \xrightarrow{j_n} B_n \xrightarrow{\pi_n} C_n \rightarrow 0$$

is exact for each n.

The Exact Sequence of Homology Theorem. If

$$0 \rightarrow A \xrightarrow{j} B \xrightarrow{\pi} C \rightarrow 0$$

is an exact sequence of complexes, it induces the following exact sequence of homology:

$$\cdots \rightarrow H_{n+1}(C) \xrightarrow{\theta} H_n(A) \xrightarrow{j_*} H_n(B) \xrightarrow{\pi_*}$$
$$H_n(C) \xrightarrow{\theta} H_{n-1}(A) \xrightarrow{j_*} H_{n-1}(B) \xrightarrow{\pi_*} H_{n-1}(C) \xrightarrow{\theta} \cdots$$

Remarks. The R homomorphisms θ are called *connecting maps*. Note that we have omitted subscripts on the connecting maps. Many proofs in this chapter involve a certain amount of "diagram chasing," and for this proof the following diagram is appropriate:

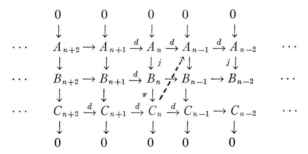

Recall that this diagram is commutative.

Proof. First we wish to define the connecting homomorphism $\theta: H_n(C) \to H_{n-1}(A)$. Note on the preceding diagram the dashed arrow from C_n to A_{n-1}. This indicates the path to follow for the construction of θ. There will be several choices involved in the construction, but after we have completed the definition, we shall show that it did not depend on these choices.

Let $x \in H_n(C)$ and choose $c \in C_n$ such that c is in the coset x. By the definition of the homology groups, we see that $d(c) = 0$. Since $B_n \xrightarrow{\pi} C_n \to 0$ is exact, there exists $b \in B_n$ such that $\pi(b) = c$. Now form $d(b) \in B_{n-1}$ and observe that, from the commutativity of the diagram, $\pi d(b) = d\pi(b) = d(c) = 0$. Since $A_{n-1} \xrightarrow{j} B_{n-1} \xrightarrow{\pi} C_{n-1}$ is exact, there exists $a \in A_{n-1}$ such that $j(a) = d(b)$. There is no arbitrary choice involved in the selection of a, since j is a monomorphism. The definition of $\theta(x)$ now emerges: Let $\theta(x)$ be the coset in $H_{n-1}(A)$ containing the element a. We note first that a is in such a coset, since $jd(a) = dj(a) = dd(b) = 0$ and the fact that j is a monomorphism imply that $d(a) = 0$.

The reader will note that in the construction of $\theta(x)$, we made two arbitrary choices, the selection of the elements b and c. In the following discussion, we shall show that $\theta(x)$ is independent of these selections.

(a) $\theta(x)$ is independent of the choice of b. Suppose that c has been selected and that b, b' have the property that $\pi(b) = \pi(b') = c$. Then, from the exactness of $A_n \xrightarrow{j} B_n \xrightarrow{\pi} C_n$, we see that $b = b' + j(a_0)$ for $a_0 \in A_n$. Applying d and a little commutativity, we see that $d(b) = d(b') + jd(a_0)$. Now suppose that we try to construct $\theta(x)$, using b' instead of b; then we obtain an (unique) element $a' \in A_{n-1}$ such that $j(a') = d(b')$. However, the above equation implies that $a = a' + d(a_0)$ and that a and a' are in the same coset mod Im d. That is, once c has been chosen, $\theta(x)$ does not depend on the choice of b.

(b) $\theta(x)$ is independent of the choice of c. Suppose that c and c' are two elements in the coset x; then $c = c' + d(c_0)$ for $c_0 \in C_{n+1}$. Since the map π is an epimorphism, there exists $b_0 \in B_{n+1}$ such that $\pi(b_0) = c_0$. The above equation can be rewritten $c = c' + \pi d(b_0)$, using the commutativity of the big diagram.

Now choose b' in B_n such that $\pi(b') = c'$. This is the b' that goes with c' in the construction of $\theta(x)$, using the element c'. Since it has been shown that once c is selected, $\theta(x)$ does not depend on the choice of b, we are free to choose any b such that $\pi(b) = c$. A judicious way to do this is to let $b = b' + d(b_0)$. By applying π to both sides, we see that this is an acceptable choice for the b to go with the c. From now on in the construction of $\theta(x)$, it is clear that we must get the same coset in $H_{n-1}(A)$ because the two elements $d(b)$ and $d(b')$ are actually equal (because $dd(b_0) = 0$).

(c) θ is an R homomorphism. If x and x' are two elements of $H_n(C)$, we can choose elements c and c', representing the cosets x and x', and $c + c'$ will represent $x + x'$. Now choose b and b' in B_n such that $\pi(b) = c$ and $\pi(b') = c'$; note that $\pi(b + b') = c + c'$. Now, using these b's and c's, one gets the equation $\theta(x + x') = \theta(x) + \theta(x')$.

To show that $r\theta(x) = \theta(rx)$ for r in the ring R, be sure to select rc to represent the coset rx if c represents x. Then select rb to map on rc by π if b has been selected so that $\pi(b) = c$. The desired equation will follow from these selections.

Now that θ has been constructed, the remainder of the proof consists of showing the exactness of the homology sequence. The reader really should attempt this on his own by running all over the big diagram. Although there are a number of steps in the proof, at any point in the proof there is really only one thing to do — and that always turns out to be the right thing. Even the construction of θ that we have just worked out, although complicated, is the only reasonable homomorphism from $H_n(C)$ to $H_{n-1}(A)$ that has any connection with the complexes.

We shall next give a proof of the exactness of the homology sequence, just for the sake of completeness, and the reader should consult this proof only if he gets stuck.

(d) Exactness at $H_{n-1}(A)$. In proving exactness, there are two things to show: $j_*\theta = 0$, and if $j_*(y) = 0$, then there exists x in $H_n(C)$ such that $\theta(x) = y$.

Let $x \in H_n(C)$ and, according to the recipe for concocting $\theta(x)$, choose c representing x, b such that $\pi(b) = c$, and choose a in A_{n-1} such that $j(a) = d(b)$. Then the element a represents the coset $\theta(x)$ in $H_{n-1}(A)$, and $j_*\theta(x)$ is the coset containing $j(a)$ in $H_{n-1}(B)$. But then $j_*\theta(x) = 0$, since $j(a) \in \operatorname{Im} d$.

Now suppose that $j_*(y) = 0$ for y in $H_{n-1}(A)$, and let $a \in H_{n-1}(A)$ be in the coset y. The statement that $j_*(y) = 0$ means that $j(a) = d(b)$ for some b in B_n. Form $\pi(b) = c \in C_n$ and let $x \in H_n(C)$ be the coset containing c. From the definition of the element $\theta(x)$, we see that $\theta(x) = y$. This completes the proof of exactness at $H_{n-1}(A)$.

(e) Exactness at $H_n(C)$. Let $b \in B_n$ be in the coset $z \in H_n(B)$; $\pi(b)$ represents $\pi_*(z)$. It is convenient to let $\pi(b) = c$ and b represent the elements c and b used to define $\theta\pi_*(z)$. But then $\theta\pi_*(z) = 0$ because $d(b) = 0$.

Suppose now that $\theta(x) = 0$ for $x \in H_n(C)$. Suppose also that the elements a, b, and c are chosen so that c represents x, $\pi(b) = c$, and $j(a) = d(b)$. Then the statement that $\theta(x) = 0$ means that $a = d(a')$ for some a' in A_n. Now let $b' = b - j(a')$. The claim is that (although $d(b)$ might not be zero) we have arranged it so that $d(b') = 0$ and $\pi(b) = \pi(b') = c$. Then we let z in $H_n(B)$ be the coset containing b', and we observe that $\pi_*(z) = x$. This completes the proof of exactness at $H_n(C)$.

(f) Exactness at $H_n(B)$. It follows from the exactness of the sequence $A_n \xrightarrow{j} B_n \xrightarrow{\pi} C_n$ that the induced maps in homology, j_* and π_*, satisfy the equation $\pi_* j_* = 0$.

Let z belong to $H_n(B)$ and suppose that $\pi_*(z) = 0$. If b is a representative of z, this means that $\pi(b) = d(c')$ for some c' in C_{n+1}. Since π is an epimorphism, there is an element b' in B_{n+1} such that $\pi(b') = c'$. Now form the element $b - d(b')$ in B_n; note that this also represents the coset z and has the additional property that $\pi(b - d(b')) = 0$. Thus, we can find $a \in A_n$ such that $j(a) = b - d(b')$, and we can also show that $d(a) = 0$, using the fact that $d(b - d(b')) = 0$. Now we let w be the coset of $H_n(A)$ containing a, and we see that $j_*(w) = z$. This completes the proof of exactness at $H_n(B)$ and also the proof of the theorem.

We remark here that the corresponding theorem for complexes with differentiation going up $(d_n: A_n \to A_{n+1})$ has the same proof. In this case, the connecting homomorphism also goes up by one $\theta: H_n(C) \to H_{n+1}(A)$.

DEFINITION. If A and B are R modules, the additive group of all R homomorphisms of A into B is denoted by Hom (A, B). When we need to emphasize the ring R, we shall write $\text{Hom}_R (A, B)$.

Suppose $f: A \to B$ is an R homomorphism, and let M be any R module. The mapping f induces two group homomorphisms

$$f': \text{Hom } (B, M) \to \text{Hom } (A, M)$$

defined by $f'(g) = gf$, for $g \in \text{Hom } (B, M)$, and

$$f'': \text{Hom } (M, A) \to \text{Hom } (M, B)$$

defined by $f''(h) = fh$, for $h \in \text{Hom } (M, A)$.

The sequence $A \xrightarrow{f} B \xrightarrow{g} C$ gives rise to the sequences

$$\text{Hom } (C, M) \xrightarrow{g'} \text{Hom } (B, M) \xrightarrow{f'} \text{Hom } (A, M)$$

and

$$\text{Hom } (M, A) \xrightarrow{f''} \text{Hom } (M, B) \xrightarrow{g''} \text{Hom } (M, C).$$

One should check to see that the relations $f'g' = (gf)'$ and $(gf)'' = g''f''$ hold for the various compositions. Observe that if $g = $ the identity map then g' and g'' are also identity maps. If

$$0 \rightarrow A \xrightarrow{j} B \xrightarrow{\pi} C \rightarrow 0 \qquad (3.1)$$

is exact, then it and the module M induce two other exact sequences:

$$0 \rightarrow \text{Hom } (C, M) \xrightarrow{\pi'} \text{Hom } (B, M) \xrightarrow{j'} \text{Hom } (A, M) \qquad (3.2)$$

and

$$0 \rightarrow \text{Hom } (M, A) \xrightarrow{j''} \text{Hom } (M, B) \xrightarrow{\pi''} \text{Hom } (M, C). \qquad (3.3)$$

Exactness at Hom (C, M) and Hom (M, A) is fairly easy; in the first case, use the fact that π is an empimorphism and in the second case, that j is a monomorphism.

To check exactness at Hom (B, M), we first note that $j'\pi' = 0$; for if $f \in \text{Hom } (C, M)$, then $j'\pi'(f) = f\pi j = 0$ because $\pi j = 0$. Finally, suppose that for $g \in \text{Hom } (B, M)$, we have $j'(g) = gj = 0$. That is, Ker $g \supseteq \text{Im } j = $ Ker π, and we can define $k: C \rightarrow M$ by the operation $k(c) = g(b)$, where $\pi(b) = a$. We observe that for every $c \in C$, there is such a $b \in B$ and that the definition of $b(c)$ is independent of the choice of such a $b \in B$. This latter statement comes from the fact that Ker $g \supseteq $ Ker π. The reader may verify that $h: C \rightarrow M$ is a homomorphism and that $h\pi = g$ is equivalently $\pi'(h) = g$. Thus, we have established exactness at Hom (B, M). Incidentally, another way to establish the existence of h in the above argument is to note that: (1) π induces an isomorphism $\bar{\pi}: B/\text{Ker } \pi \rightarrow C$; (2) g induces a homomorphism $\bar{g}: B/\text{Ker } \pi \rightarrow M$; and (3) $h = \bar{g}\bar{\pi}^{-1}$.

The method for showing exactness at Hom (M, B) is analogous. First observe that $\pi''j'' = 0$ because $\pi j = 0$. Then choose $h \in \text{Hom } (M, B)$ so that $\pi'(h) = 0$. This implies that Im $h \subseteq \text{Im } j = $ Ker π. Since j is a monomorphism, it induces an isomorphism $j: A \rightarrow \text{Im } j$, and we can define $f: M \rightarrow A$ by the equation $f = j^{-1}h$. The reader may check to see that $j''(f) = h$. Thus, we have exactness at Hom (M, B).

If, in addition to being exact, the sequence (3.1) is split exact, then (3.2) and (3.3) can be extended to

$$0 \rightarrow \text{Hom } (C, M) \xrightarrow{\pi'} \text{Hom } (B, M) \xrightarrow{j'} \text{Hom } (A, M) \rightarrow 0 \qquad (3.2')$$

and

$$0 \rightarrow \text{Hom } (M, A) \xrightarrow{j''} \text{Hom } (M, B) \xrightarrow{\pi''} \text{Hom } (M, C) \rightarrow 0 \qquad (3.3')$$

and these are also split exact.

In fact, one can use the splitting of (3.1) to produce the splitting of (3.2') or (3.3'). For example, if (3.1) is split by $k: B \rightarrow A$ such that $kj = $ identity on A, then $j'k'$ will be identity on Hom (A, M). It follows that j' is an epimorphism and that k' produces a splitting in (3.2'). The same sort of arguments hold for (3.3').

The reader will observe that P is projective if and only if, for every exact sequence $A \xrightarrow{f} B \to 0$, the induced sequence

$$\text{Hom } (P, A) \xrightarrow{f''} \text{Hom } (P, B) \to 0$$

is exact. Another way to phrase this is: "P is projective if and only if Hom $(P, \cdot)$ applied to short exact sequences gives short exact sequences." A similar argument at the other end allows one to say: "Q is injective if and only if Hom $(\cdot, Q)$ applied to short exact sequences gives short exact sequences."

DEFINITION. A projective resolution of the R module A is an exact sequence,

$$\cdots \to P_n \xrightarrow{d_n} P_{n-1} \to \cdots \to P_1 \xrightarrow{d_1} P_0 \xrightarrow{\epsilon} A \to 0,$$

with each P_i projective. Since any R module is the image of a free (and hence projective) R module, every R module has a projective resolution.

DEFINITION. Let A and C be R modules and P_n be a projective resolution of A. Consider the sequence

$$0 \to \text{Hom } (P_0, C) \xrightarrow{d_1'} \text{Hom } (P_1, C) \xrightarrow{d_2'} \cdots.$$

Since $d_{n+1}' d_n'(f) = d_{n+1}'(fd_n) = fd_n d_{n+1} = 0$ for $f \in \text{Hom } (P_{n-1}, C)$, this sequence is a complex. The nth homology group Ker $d_{n+1}'/\text{Im } d_n'$ is denoted by Ext^n (A, C).

At this point we should designate these homology groups with a P to indicate the resolution of A used to define them. However, in the following discussion, we shall show that Ext^n (A, C) does not depend on the particular projective resolution used to define it. In order to do this, we must first introduce some more notions. If we have an R homomorphism $f: A \to B$ and projective resolutions of A and B,

$$\begin{array}{ccccccc}
\cdots & P_1 \to & P_0 & \xrightarrow{\epsilon} & A \to 0 \\
& \downarrow f_1 & \downarrow f_0 & & \downarrow f \\
\cdots & \bar{P}_1 \to & \bar{P}_0 & \xrightarrow{\epsilon} & B \to 0,
\end{array}$$

then we can fill in the diagram by a series of vertical maps f_n so that the resulting diagram is commutative. Define $f_0: P_0 \to \bar{P}_0$ so that $\bar{\epsilon}f_0 = f\epsilon$ (this uses projectivity of P_0). Suppose now that f_n has been defined and that commutativity occurs up to that point. It follows that $\bar{d}_n f_n d_{n+1} = 0$; so, Im $d_n f_n \subseteq$ Im $\bar{d}_{n+1}$. The projectivity of P_{n+1} then implies that there is f_{n+1} such that

$\bar{d}_{n+1}f_{n+1} = f_n d_{n+1}$. Having filled in the above diagram, we Hom it into C and get the big diagram, which is still commutative:

$$0 \to \text{Hom } (P_0, C) \to \text{Hom } (P_1, C) \to \cdots$$
$$\downarrow f_0' \qquad\qquad \downarrow f_1'$$
$$0 \to \text{Hom } (\bar{P}_0, C) \to \text{Hom } (\bar{P}_1, C) \to \cdots$$

and in this way we induce the maps in homology

$$f^n\colon \text{Ext}^n (B, C) \to \text{Ext}^n (A, C).$$

Note again that we should have indicated that these Ext's depend on the resolutions. If the reader will just hold his breath for one more minute, we shall show that this is not necessary.

Lemma. If $f\colon A \to B$ is an R homomorphism, then the induced maps $f^n\colon \text{Ext}^n (B, C) \to \text{Ext}^n (A, C)$ are independent of choices of the f_n used to define them.

Proof. Suppose we have resolutions and maps in the commutative diagram with exact rows,

$$\cdots \quad P_1 \xrightarrow{d_1} P_0 \xrightarrow{\epsilon} A \to 0$$
$$\downarrow f_1 \quad \downarrow f_0 \quad \downarrow f$$
$$\cdots \quad \bar{P}_1 \xrightarrow{\bar{d}_1} \bar{P}_0 \xrightarrow{\bar{\epsilon}} B \to 0,$$

used in defining the induced maps of $\text{Ext}^n (B, C)$ to $\text{Ext}^n (A, C)$. To show that the induced maps are independent of the choice of the f_i, it will be enough to consider the case $f = 0$ and show in this case that it induces only the zero homomorphism of $\text{Ext}^n (B, C)$ to $\text{Ext}^n (A, C)$; for, this is equivalent to saying that if $f = g$, $f^n = g^n$ regardless of all the choices that go into their definition. By induction we define maps $D_i\colon P_i \to \bar{P}_{i+1}$ with the properties that

$$f_i = \bar{d}_{i+1}D_i + D_{i-1}d_i, \qquad i \geq 1.$$

Since $\bar{\epsilon}f_0 = f\epsilon = 0$, $\text{Im } f_0 \subseteq \text{Ker } \epsilon$. The projectivity of P_0 allows us to define $D_0\colon P_0 \to \bar{P}_1$ such that $f_0 = \bar{d}_1 D_0$. Now form $f_1 - D_0 d_1$ and observe that $\bar{d}_1(f_1 - D_0 d_1) = \bar{d}_1 f_1 - \bar{d}_1 D_0 d_1 = 0$. Thus $\text{Im } (f_1 - D_0 d_1) \subseteq \text{Ker } d_1 = \text{Im } \bar{d}_2$, and the projectivity of P_1 allows us to define $D_1\colon P_1 \to \bar{P}_2$ such that $\bar{d}_2 D_1 = f_1 - D_0 d_1$. Thus, we have pushed the definition of the D_n's as far as 1.

Assume now that D_n has been defined for $n \geq 1$, satisfying the above condition and form $f_{n+1} - D_n d_{n+1}$. As in the case of $n = 1$, notice that $\bar{d}_{n+1}(f_{n+1} - D_n d_{n+1}) = 0$ by using the property of D_n. Thus,

$$\text{Im}(f_{n+1} - D_n d_{n+1}) \subseteq \text{Im } \bar{d}_{n+2},$$

and the projectivity of P_{n+1} allows us to define $D_{n+1}: P_{n+1} \to \bar{P}_{n+2}$ such that $\bar{d}_{n+2}D_{n+1} = f_{n+1} - D_n d_{n+1}$. By induction we can define the D's all the way out. Now Hom everything in sight into C to obtain the diagram:

$$0 \to \text{Hom } (A,C) \xrightarrow{e'} \text{Hom } (P_0,C) \xrightarrow{d'_1} \cdots \text{Hom } (P_{n-1},C) \xrightarrow{d'_n} \text{Hom } (P_n,C) \xrightarrow{d'_{n+1}} \text{Hom } (P_{n+1},C) \cdots$$

At the left-hand end we see by the definition of $\text{Ext}^0 (A, C)$ and $\text{Ext}^0 (B, C)$ that we have the following commutative diagram with exact rows:

$$0 \to \text{Hom } (A, C) \xrightarrow{e'} \text{Ext}^0 (A, C) \to 0$$
$$0 \to \text{Hom } (B, C) \xrightarrow{e'} \text{Ext}^0(B, C) \to 0$$

This proves our assertion for $n = 0$. Now examine the diagram for $n \geq 1$. Note that we can still claim the relation

$$f'_n = D'_n \bar{d}'_{n+1} + d'_n D'_{n-1}.$$

Now suppose $x \in \text{Hom } (\bar{P}_n, C)$ satisfies $d'_{n+1}(x) = 0$; that is, x represents a coset of $\text{Ext}^n (B, C)$. Form $f'_n(x) = D'_n \bar{d}'_{n+1}(x) + d'_n D'_{n-1}(x) = d'_n D'_{n-1}(x)$, and note that $f'_n(x) \subseteq \text{Im } d'_n \subseteq \text{Hom } (P_n, C)$. Thus, f'_n induces the zero map from $\text{Ext}^n (B, C)$ to $\text{Ext}^n (A, C)$, and the assertion holds for all n.

THEOREM (Independence of the Resolution). If $\{P_n\}$ and $\{\bar{P}_n\}$ are two projective resolutions of A, with $\text{Ext}^n (A, C)$ and $\overline{\text{Ext}^n} (A, C)$ computed with these resolutions, then

$$\text{Ext}^n (A, C) \cong \overline{\text{Ext}^n} (A, C).$$

Proof. Use the preceding lemma on the following diagram:

$$\begin{array}{ccccccc}
\cdots & P_n & \cdots & P_1 \to P_0 \to A \to 0 \\
& g_n \downarrow & & g_1 \downarrow \quad g_0 \downarrow \quad i \downarrow \\
\cdots & \bar{P}_n & \cdots & \bar{P}_1 \to \bar{P}_0 \to A \to 0 \\
& f_n \downarrow & & f_1 \downarrow \quad f_0 \downarrow \quad i \downarrow \\
\cdots & P_n & \cdots & P_1 \to P_0 \to A \to 0
\end{array}$$

where the i's are identity maps and the f_n's and g_n's are filled in so as to get a commutative diagram. We contend that a little handwaving over the preceding lemma allows us to claim that the induced maps f^n and g^n satisfy

$$f^n g^n = \text{identity on } \overline{\text{Ext}^n} (A, C)$$

and

$$g^n f^n = \text{identity on } \text{Ext}^n (A, C).$$

The reason for one equation is that the diagram

$$
\begin{array}{ccccccccc}
\cdots & P_n & \cdots & & P_1 & \to & P_0 & \to A \to 0 \\
 & \downarrow f_n g_n & & & \downarrow f_1 g_1 & & \downarrow f_0 g_0 & \downarrow i \\
\cdots & P_n & \cdots & & P_1 & \to & P_0 & \to A \to 0
\end{array}
$$

could have been filled out all the way by identity maps on the P_n's. Thus, the composed maps must induce the identity $\text{Ext}^n (A, C)$. The other equation follows analogously.

We remark that we could do the whole thing over with two resolutions of some module E, and if we had an R homomorphism h from A to E, we should get a diagram

$$
\begin{array}{ccc}
\text{Ext}^n (A, C) & \cong & \overline{\text{Ext}}{}^n (A, C) \\
\downarrow h_n & & \downarrow h_n \\
\text{Ext}^n (E, C) & \cong & \overline{\text{Ext}}{}^n (E, C),
\end{array}
$$

which is commutative. This follows from the fact that the two horizontal isomorphisms are induced by the identities on A and E, respectively.

Another consequence of the lemma preceding the independence of resolution theorem is the relation

$$(fh)^n = h^n f^n,$$

where $h: A \to B$ and $f: B \to D$, and the characters with n's on them are the induced maps on the Ext's. The lemma allows us, in defining $(fh)^n$, to choose with considerable freedom the maps $(fh)_n$ from the nth projective in a resolution of A. If we are clever, we shall let $(fh)_n = f_n h_n$, where the f_n and h_n have already been selected in order to define f^n and h^n. The above equation will then follow.

Let us now turn our attention to the C in the group $\text{Ext}^n (A, C)$. Suppose that

$$\cdots P_n \xrightarrow{d_n} \cdots P_1 \xrightarrow{d_1} P_0 \xrightarrow{\varepsilon} A \to 0$$

is a projective resolution of A and if $C \xrightarrow{g} D$ is an R homomorphism, we get the commutative diagram

$$
\begin{array}{ccccc}
0 \to \text{Hom} (P_0, C) & \xrightarrow{d_1} & \text{Hom} (P_1, C) & \cdots \\
\downarrow g'' & & \downarrow g'' & \\
0 \to \text{Hom} (P_0, D) & \xrightarrow{d'_1} & \text{Hom} (P_1, D) & \cdots.
\end{array}
$$

Thus, the maps g'' induce g^n: $\text{Ext}^n(A, C) \to \text{Ext}^n(A, D)$. At this point, we suggest that the reader examine the proof of the uniqueness of $\text{Ext}^n(A, C)$ and note that the corresponding diagrams and proof with C replaced by D remain valid. But the proof for C and the proof for D can be pasted together with g'': $\text{Hom}(X, C) \to \text{Hom}(X, D)$ for every X that occurred in the theorem, and the new jumbo diagrams will still commute. We claim this proves that the diagram

$$
\begin{array}{ccc}
\text{Ext}^n(A, C) & \xrightarrow{g^n} & \text{Ext}^n(A, D) \\
\wr\| & & \wr\| \\
\overline{\text{Ext}}^n(A, C) & \xrightarrow{g^n} & \overline{\text{Ext}}^n(A, D)
\end{array}
$$

is commutative, where the bar over Ext is from the notation of the theorem and the vertical isomorphisms are as shown in that theorem. That is, we believe we have outlined the proof of the following theorem.

THEOREM. If $g: C \to D$ is an R homomorphism, it induces g^n: $\text{Ext}^n(A, C) \to \text{Ext}^n(A, D)$, and the mappings g^n are independent of the resolutions used to define Ext.

There are some properties of the mappings g^n that follow rather easily from the definition. If $C \xrightarrow{g} D$ and $D \xrightarrow{h} E$ are homomorphisms, then $(hg)^n = h^n g^n$. Also, it is clear that if i is the identity on C, then i^n is the identity on $\text{Ext}^n(A, C)$.

Perhaps this would be a good place to pause and reflect on the nature of Ext as we have developed it so far. For a fixed module C and integer n, we have an expression $\text{Ext}^n(\cdot, C)$, which when applied to modules A gives abelian groups $\text{Ext}^n(A, C)$. One can think of this as a function with a class of modules for a domain and a class of abelian groups for a range. Strictly speaking, it is not a function because the domain and range are not sets, but the analogy is fairly close.

If we examine the situation closely, we note that the above description of Ext does not take into account the induced mappings f^n. In fact, if we adopt the following suggestive (and cumbersome) notation, it might give the reader a better idea of what is going on. If $f: A \to B$ induces f^n: $\text{Ext}^n(B, C) \to \text{Ext}^n(A, C)$, suppose we designate f^n by $\text{Ext}^n(f, C)$. This notation emphasizes the fact that the induced map f^n depends on C.

Now we see that we really have something like a function that, when applied to modules and mappings, gives abelian groups and mappings. This is an example of what is called a *functor*.

If $\mathfrak{C}$ is a class of modules and maps and $\mathfrak{D}$ is a class of modules and maps, we shall say that $F: \mathfrak{C} \to \mathfrak{D}$ is a *contravariant functor* if, for all A, B, modules in $\mathfrak{C}$ and f, a map $A \xrightarrow{f} B$, there exists $F(A)$, $F(B)$ modules in $\mathfrak{D}$ and $F(f)$, a map in $\mathfrak{D}$, such that $F(f): F(B) \to F(A)$. We also require that F satisfy the following rules:

(1) F applied to the commutative diagram

$$\begin{array}{c} B \\ {}^{f}\nearrow \quad \searrow^{g} \\ A \xrightarrow[gf]{} C \end{array}$$

gives the commutative diagram

$$\begin{array}{c} F(B) \\ {}_{F(f)}\swarrow \quad \nwarrow_{F(g)} \\ F(A) \xleftarrow[F(gf)]{} F(C) \end{array}$$

(2) If $i: A \to A$ is the identity map on A, then $F(i)$ is the identity map on $F(A)$.

Observe that this is enough to deduce that if A is isomorphic to B, then $F(A)$ is isomorphic to $F(B)$. In fact, if $\theta: A \to B$ is an isomorphism, then so is $F(\theta): F(B) \to F(A)$. As an example of a contravariant functor, we have $\text{Ext}^n (\cdot C)$.

The functor G from $\mathfrak{C}$ to $\mathfrak{D}$ is called a *covariant functor* if $A \xrightarrow{f} B$ for modules and maps in $\mathfrak{C}$ gives $G(A) \xrightarrow{G(f)} G(B)$ modules and maps in $\mathfrak{D}$. We require that G satisfy the rule 2, and the following rule

(1') G applied to the commutative diagram

$$\begin{array}{c} B \\ {}^{f}\nearrow \quad \searrow^{g} \\ A \xrightarrow[gf]{} C \end{array}$$

gives the commutative diagram

$$\begin{array}{c} G(B) \\ {}_{C(f)}\nearrow \quad \searrow_{G(g)} \\ G(A) \xrightarrow[G(gf)]{} G(C) \end{array}$$

All the functors F that we consider have the additional property that F applied to the zero module is the zero module.

A functor H is called an *exact functor* if it preserves exact sequences. That is, if $0 \to A \to B \to C \to 0$ is an exact sequence, then $0 \to H(A) \to H(B) \to H(C) \to 0$ (or $0 \to H(C) \to H(B) \to H(A) \to 0$ if H is contravariant) is also exact. As we noted earlier, the functor Hom $(\cdot Q)$ with injective Q is an exact contravariant functor and Hom $(P \cdot)$ with projective P is an exact covariant functor. It is not hard to show that if a functor is exact, then it preserves long exact sequences as well as short ones.

We shall say that two functors F, H from $\mathfrak{C}$ to $\mathfrak{D}$ are *equivalent* if, for each module A in $\mathfrak{C}$, $F(A)$ and $H(A)$ are isomorphic by an isomorphism θ so that the map $A \xrightarrow{f} B$ induces a commutative diagram

$$
\begin{array}{ccc}
F(A) & \xrightarrow{F(f)} & F(B) \\
\wr\|\theta & & \wr\|\theta \\
H(A) & \xrightarrow{H(f)} & H(B)
\end{array}
$$

That is, not only must $F(A)$ and $H(A)$ be isomorphic for all A, but the isomorphisms must commute with the maps $H(f)$ and $F(f)$. Note that in the two preceding theorems we were showing that the functors Ext and $\overline{\text{Ext}}$ arising from two different projective resolutions are equivalent functors. We shall consider equivalent functors as essentially the same.

Let us now return to Ext (and to the sloppy but short notation f^n for the induced maps in Ext). We shall use the following theorem in developing the homology sequence for Ext.

Simultaneous Resolution Theorem. If

$$
0 \to A \xrightarrow{j} B \xrightarrow{\pi} C \to 0
$$

is exact, and if P_i and $\bar{P}_i$ are projective resolutions of A and C, respectively, then there exists a projective resolution of B such that the following diagram is commutative,

$$
\begin{array}{ccccccc}
& 0 & & 0 & & 0 & & 0 \\
& \downarrow & & \downarrow & & \downarrow & & \downarrow \\
\cdots & P_2 & \to & P_1 & \to & P_0 & \to A \to 0 \\
& \downarrow & & \downarrow & & \downarrow & & \downarrow \\
\cdots & P_2 \oplus \bar{P}_2 & \to & P_1 \oplus \bar{P}_1 & \to & P_0 \oplus \bar{P}_0 & \to B \to 0 \\
& \downarrow & & \downarrow & & \downarrow & & \downarrow \\
\cdots & \bar{P}_2 & \to & \bar{P}_1 & \to & \bar{P}_0 & \to C \to 0 \\
& \downarrow & & \downarrow & & \downarrow & & \downarrow \\
& 0 & & 0 & & 0 & & 0
\end{array}
$$

with exact rows and columns and the columns of P's are split exact.

Proof. We start building the middle resolution one step at a time Consider the following diagram. Given the diagram of solid arrows,

$$
\begin{array}{ccc}
0 & 0 \\
\downarrow & \downarrow \\
P_0 \xrightarrow{\epsilon} A \to 0 \\
\downarrow{\scriptstyle j_0} \quad \downarrow{\scriptstyle j} \\
P_0 \oplus \bar{P}_0 \xrightarrow{\epsilon'} B \to 0 \\
\downarrow{\scriptstyle \pi_0}\nearrow{\scriptstyle \mu} \downarrow{\scriptstyle \pi} \\
\bar{P}_0 \underset{\bar{\epsilon}}{\rightrightarrows} C \to 0 \\
\downarrow \quad \downarrow \\
0 \quad 0
\end{array}
$$

we fill in the dashed arrows as follows: There exists $\mu \colon \bar{P}_0 \to B$ such that $\pi\mu = \bar{\epsilon}$, since $\bar{P}_0$ is projective. Now define the following homomorphisms for $p \in P_0,\ \bar{p} \in \bar{P}_0$:

$$j_0 \colon P_0 \to P_0 \oplus \bar{P}_0 \qquad \text{by } j_0(p) = (p, 0),$$

$$\pi_0 \colon P_0 \oplus \bar{P}_0 \to \bar{P}_0 \qquad \text{by } \pi_0(p, \bar{p}) = \bar{p} \text{ (projection on 2nd component)},$$

$$\epsilon' \colon P_0 \oplus \bar{P}_0 \to B \qquad \text{by } \epsilon'(p, \bar{p}) = j\epsilon(p) + \mu(\bar{p}).$$

These are all homomorphisms, and one checks to see that the squares commute by direct computation. This is left to the reader.

We shall verify that ϵ' is an epimorphism. Let $b \in B$; then $\pi(b) \in C$ and there exists $\bar{p} \in \bar{P}$ such that $\bar{\epsilon}(\bar{p}) = \pi(b)$. It follows that $\pi(b - \mu(\bar{p})) = 0$, so that $b - \mu(\bar{p}) = j\epsilon(p)$ for a suitable $p \in P_0$. Then we see that $\epsilon'(p, \bar{p}) = b$. Thus, ϵ' is an epimorphism.

Now we claim that the above diagram induces a commutative diagram with exact rows and columns,

$$
\begin{array}{ccccc}
0 & & 0 & & 0 \\
\downarrow & & \downarrow & & \downarrow \\
0 \to \mathrm{Ker}\ \epsilon \to & & P_0 & \xrightarrow{\epsilon} A \to 0 \\
\downarrow & & {\scriptstyle j_0}\downarrow & & \downarrow{\scriptstyle j} \\
0 \to \mathrm{Ker}\ \epsilon' \to & P_0 \oplus \bar{P}_0 & \underset{\epsilon'}{\rightarrow} B \to 0 \\
\downarrow & & {\scriptstyle \pi_0}\downarrow & & \downarrow{\scriptstyle \pi} \\
0 \to \mathrm{Ker}\ \bar{\epsilon} \to & & \bar{P}_0 & \underset{\bar{\epsilon}}{\rightrightarrows} C \to 0 \\
\downarrow & & \downarrow & & \downarrow \\
0 & & 0 & & 0
\end{array}
$$

where the monomorphisms on the left are just the injections of the kernels into the column of P's, and the homomorphisms in the left are the restrictions of those in the center column. The verification of this claim is a direct computation, using the definitions of the various maps. We leave this computation to the reader. This completes the first step of the construction of large diagrams in the conclusion.

It is also an outline of the construction at the nth step; for, suppose that the construction has been carried this far

$$
\begin{array}{c}
0 \\
\downarrow \\
P_n \xrightarrow{\delta_n} P_{n-1} \xrightarrow{\delta_{n-1}} \cdots \\
\downarrow {\scriptstyle j_{n-1}} \\
P_{n-1} \oplus \bar{P}_{n-1} \xrightarrow{\delta'_{n-1}} \cdots \\
\downarrow {\scriptstyle \pi_{n-1}} \\
P_n \xrightarrow{\bar{\delta}_n} P_{n-1} \xrightarrow{\bar{\delta}_{n-1}} \cdots \\
\downarrow \\
0
\end{array}
$$

and that the sequence of kernels,

$$0 \to \operatorname{Ker} \delta_{n-1} \to \operatorname{Ker} \delta'_{n-1} \to \operatorname{Ker} \bar{\delta}_{n-1} \to 0,$$

is exact. Then we can perform the process outlined above on

$$
\begin{array}{c}
0 \\
\downarrow \\
P_n \xrightarrow{\delta_n} \operatorname{Ker} \delta_{n-1} \to 0 \\
\downarrow \\
\operatorname{Ker} \delta'_{n-1} \to 0 \\
\downarrow \\
\bar{P}_n \xrightarrow{\delta_n} \operatorname{Ker} \bar{\delta}_{n-1} \to 0 \\
\downarrow \\
0
\end{array}
$$

and obtain j_n, π_n, δ'_n, and an exact sequence of kernels:

$$0 \to \operatorname{Ker} \delta_n \to \operatorname{Ker} \delta'_n \to \operatorname{Ker} \bar{\delta}_n \to 0.$$

This completes the inductive step and the proof of the theorem.

We complete this chapter with the examination of two exact sequences of homology that occur in the two variables of Ext. These two theorems are the most important in the chapter because they will be used repeatedly in later chapters.

Theorem (Exact Sequence in the First Variable of Ext). If

$$0 \to A \xrightarrow{j} B \xrightarrow{\pi} D \to 0$$

is exact, it induces the exact sequence

$$\cdots \operatorname{Ext}^{n-1}(A, C) \xrightarrow{\theta} \operatorname{Ext}^n(D, C) \xrightarrow{\pi^n} \operatorname{Ext}^n(B, C)$$
$$\xrightarrow{j^n} \operatorname{Ext}^n(A, C) \xrightarrow{\theta} \operatorname{Ext}^{n+1}(D, C) \cdots.$$

Proof. Resolve A and D with projective resolutions and apply the theorem on simultaneous resolutions to obtain resolutions of A, B, and D hooked together as in that theorem:

$$
\begin{array}{ccccc}
& 0 & & 0 & 0 \\
& \downarrow & & \downarrow & \downarrow \\
\cdots & P_1 & \rightarrow & P_0 & \rightarrow A \rightarrow 0 \\
& \downarrow & & \downarrow & \downarrow j \\
\cdots & P_1 \oplus \bar{P}_1 & \rightarrow & P_0 \oplus \bar{P}_0 & \rightarrow B \rightarrow 0 \\
& \downarrow & & \downarrow & \downarrow \pi \\
\cdots & \bar{P}_1 & \rightarrow & \bar{P}_0 & \rightarrow D \rightarrow 0 \\
& \downarrow & & \downarrow & \downarrow \\
& 0 & & 0 & 0
\end{array}
$$

Now Hom every projective in sight into C to get the following exact sequence of complexes:

$$
\begin{array}{ccccc}
& 0 & & 0 & 0 \\
& \uparrow & & \uparrow & \uparrow \\
0 \rightarrow \mathrm{Hom}\,(P_0, C) & \rightarrow & \mathrm{Hom}\,(P_1, C) & \rightarrow & \mathrm{Hom}\,(P_2, C) \quad \cdots \\
& \uparrow & & \uparrow & \uparrow \\
0 \rightarrow \mathrm{Hom}\,(P_0 \oplus \bar{P}_0, C) & \rightarrow & \mathrm{Hom}\,(P_1 \oplus \bar{P}_1, C) & \rightarrow & \mathrm{Hom}\,(P_2 \oplus \bar{P}_2, C) \quad \cdots \\
& \uparrow & & \uparrow & \uparrow \\
0 \rightarrow \mathrm{Hom}\,(\bar{P}_0, C) & \rightarrow & \mathrm{Hom}\,(\bar{P}_1, C) & \rightarrow & \mathrm{Hom}\,(\bar{P}_2, C) \quad \cdots \\
& \uparrow & & \uparrow & \uparrow \\
& 0 & & 0 & 0
\end{array}
$$

where the vertical sequences are split exact, since the original sequences of P's were split exact.

Observe now that the diagram we have just constructed is an exact sequence of the very complexes used to compute $\mathrm{Ext}^n\,(D, C)$, $\mathrm{Ext}^n\,(B, C)$, and $\mathrm{Ext}^n\,(A, C)$; by the exact sequence of homology theorem, these are strung together in just the conclusion of the theorem. Note also that the induced j^n, π^n are just what they ought to be. This completes the proof of the theorem.

Theorem (Exact Sequence in the Second Variable of Ext). If

$$
0 \rightarrow C \xrightarrow{j} E \xrightarrow{\pi} F \rightarrow 0
$$

is exact, it induces the following exact sequence:

$$
\cdots \quad \mathrm{Ext}^{n-1}\,(A, F) \xrightarrow{\theta} \mathrm{Ext}^n\,(A, C) \xrightarrow{j^n} \mathrm{Ext}^n\,(A, E)
$$
$$
\xrightarrow{\pi^n} \mathrm{Ext}^n\,(A, F) \xrightarrow{\theta} \mathrm{Ext}^{n+1}\,(A, C) \quad \cdots.
$$

Proof. First form a projective resolution of A,

$$\cdots P_n \cdots P_1 \xrightarrow{d} P_0 \xrightarrow{\epsilon} A \to 0$$

and Hom all the projectives into C, E, and F, filling in with j'' and π'' where possible to get the following diagram:

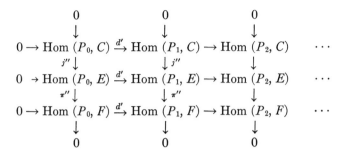

We can claim that the vertical sequences are exact, on the basis of the remark made several pages back, namely, that "Hom $(P, \cdot)$ sends short exact sequences to short exact sequences when P is projective." The commutativity of the above diagram is really a consequence of the fact that functional composition is associative. That is, if $f \in$ Hom (P_0, C), then $j''d'(f) = jfd$ and $d'j''(f) = jfd$, and these are equal. Commutativity in other squares uses the same argument.

The diagram we have constructed is an exact sequence of complexes, exactly those complexes used in the construction of the Ext's that appear in the conclusion of the theorem. In fact the conclusion of the theorem is the exact sequence of homology of this exact sequence of complexes.

Theorem (Splitting of Ext). If

$$0 \to A \xrightarrow{j} B \xrightarrow{\pi} D \to 0$$

is exact and splits, then for each n and C,

$$0 \to \text{Ext}^n (D, C) \xrightarrow{\pi^n} \text{Ext}^n (B, C) \xrightarrow{j^n} \text{Ext}^n (A, C) \to 0$$

is exact and splits.

Proof. Suppose that ρ gives the splitting, that is, $\pi\rho$ is identity on D. Then we can construct k so that kj is identity on A. But then $j^n k^n$ is identity on $\text{Ext}^n (A, C)$ and $\rho^n \pi^n$ is identity on $\text{Ext}^n (D, C)$. These facts, together with the exact sequence of homology in the first variable, give the desired exactness and splitting in the conclusion of the theorem.

We state the corresponding theorem in the second variable.

THEOREM. If $0 \to C \xrightarrow{j} E \xrightarrow{\pi} F \to 0$ is exact and split, then

$$0 \to \mathrm{Ext}^n \, (A, C) \xrightarrow{j^n} \mathrm{Ext}^n \, (A, E) \xrightarrow{\pi^n} \mathrm{Ext}^n \, (A, F) \to 0$$

is also split exact.

Proof. The proof is so close to the preceding proof that we leave it to the reader to fill it in.

Perhaps this is a good time to point out the connection between Hom and Ext^0. It is quite possible that the reader has already noticed this connection, that is, that Hom (A, C) is isomorphic to $\mathrm{Ext}^0 \, (A, C)$. Or, using the notion of functor, the functor Hom $(\cdot C)$ is equivalent to $\mathrm{Ext}^0 \, (\cdot C)$ and Hom $(A \cdot)$ is equivalent to $\mathrm{Ext}^0 \, (A \cdot)$. In the following discussion, we shall establish this. Let

$$0 \to C \xrightarrow{j} E \xrightarrow{\pi} F \to 0$$

be exact. Resolve A with P_n and form

$$
\begin{array}{ccccc}
0 & & 0 & & 0 \\
\downarrow & & \downarrow & & \downarrow \\
0 \to \mathrm{Hom} \, (A, C) \xrightarrow{\varepsilon'} & \mathrm{Hom} \, (P_0, C) \xrightarrow{d_1'} & \mathrm{Hom} \, (P_1, C) & \cdots \\
\downarrow j'' & & \downarrow & & \downarrow \\
0 \to \mathrm{Hom} \, (A, E) \to & \mathrm{Hom} \, (P_0, E) \to & \mathrm{Hom} \, (P_1, E) & \cdots \\
\downarrow \pi'' & & \downarrow & & \downarrow \\
0 \to \mathrm{Hom} \, (A, F) \to & \mathrm{Hom} \, (P_0, F) \to & \mathrm{Hom} \, (P_1, F) & \cdots \\
\downarrow & & \downarrow & & \downarrow \\
0 & & 0 & & 0
\end{array}
$$

All columns are exact, and the diagram is commutative. This diagram induces another:

$$
\begin{array}{l}
0 \to \mathrm{Hom} \, (A, C) \xrightarrow{j''} \mathrm{Hom} \, (A, E) \xrightarrow{\pi''} \mathrm{Hom} \, (A, F) \\
\qquad \| \qquad\qquad\qquad\ \| \qquad\qquad\qquad\ \| \\
0 \to \mathrm{Ext}^0 \, (A, C) \xrightarrow{j^0} \mathrm{Ext}^0 \, (A, E) \xrightarrow{\pi^0} \mathrm{Ext}^0 \, (A, F) \xrightarrow{\theta} \mathrm{Ext}^1 \, (A, C) \quad \cdots .
\end{array}
$$

This latter diagram is commutative, and we see that the exact sequence of homology in the second variable of Ext starts out with the sequence of Hom's. Thus, $\mathrm{Ext}^0 \, (A, C)$ is really our old friend Hom (A, C). Moreover, from the commutativity of the preceding diagram, after identifying various Hom's with the corresponding Ext^0's, we see that the induced map j'' corresponds to j^0 and π'' corresponds to π^0. From now on we shall think of the exact sequence of homology in the second variable of Ext as beginning with

$$0 \to \mathrm{Hom} \, (A, C) \xrightarrow{j''} \mathrm{Hom} \, (A, E) \xrightarrow{\pi''} \mathrm{Hom} \, (A, F) \xrightarrow{\theta} \mathrm{Ext}^1 \, (A, C) \quad \cdots .$$

A similar argument works in the first variable. That is, if

$$0 \to A \to B \to D \to 0$$

is exact, then one can deduce a commutative diagram:

$$0 \to \mathrm{Hom}\,(D, C) \xrightarrow{\pi'} \mathrm{Hom}\,(B, C) \xrightarrow{j'} \mathrm{Hom}\,(A, C)$$
$$\wr\| \qquad\qquad \wr\| \qquad\qquad \wr\|$$
$$0 \to \mathrm{Ext}^0\,(D, C) \xrightarrow{\pi^0} \mathrm{Ext}^0\,(B, C) \xrightarrow{j^0} \mathrm{Ext}^0\,(A, C) \xrightarrow{\theta} \mathrm{Ext}^1\,(D, C) \quad \cdots.$$

We invite the reader to try this. The trick is to resolve A, B, and D according to the simultaneous resolution theorem, Hom everything (including A, B, and D) into C, and then notice how Hom is hooked up with Ext^0 in the diagram.

It is high time we actually computed Ext of something so we do that with the following lemma.

Lemma 1. $\mathrm{Ext}^1\,(A, C) = 0$ for all C if and only if A is projective.

Proof. If A is projective, it has a projective resolution

$$0 \to A \xrightarrow{i} A \to 0,$$

and if $\mathrm{Ext}^1\,(A, C)$ is computed according to this, we see that $\mathrm{Ext}^1\,(A, C) = 0$. Note also that $\mathrm{Ext}^n\,(A, C) = 0$ for all $n \geq 1$.
 Conversely, if $\mathrm{Ext}^1\,(A, C) = 0$ for all C, and if

$$0 \to C \to E \xrightarrow{\pi} F \to 0$$

is exact, then by the exact sequence in the second variable we have that

$$0 \to \mathrm{Hom}\,(A, C) \to \mathrm{Hom}\,(A, E) \xrightarrow{\pi''} \mathrm{Hom}\,(A, F) \xrightarrow{\theta} \mathrm{Ext}^1\,(A, C)$$

is exact. But this says that π'' is an epimorphism — which, holding for all $E \xrightarrow{\pi} F \to 0$, is just another way of saying that A is projective.
 Note that the first part of the lemma implies $\mathrm{Ext}^n\,(A, C) = 0$ for all C and all $n \geq 1$ if A is projective. We may then restate the lemma in another form.

Lemma 2. $\mathrm{Ext}^n\,(A, C) = 0$ for all C and $n \geq 1$ if and only if A is projective.

Lemma 2 immediately suggests a way of describing semisimple rings with minimum conditions in terms of Ext. The following theorem states a condition that could have been tacked onto the main structure theorem of the preceding chapter.
THEOREM. The ring R is a semisimple ring with minimum condition if and

only if for every pair of R modules A and C and for every integer $n \geq 1$
$\mathrm{Ext}^n (A, C) = 0$.

Proof. From Lemma 2, it is clear that the condition of the theorem is equivalent to every R module being projective, which is one of the conditions in the main structure theorem of the preceding chapter.

EXERCISES

In the following exercises assume that R has minimum condition on left ideals.

1. Let N be the radical of R (see Exercises at the end of Chapter 2 for definition). Show that if f is in Hom (A, B), then $f(NA) \subseteq NB$.

2. Show that if $NC = 0$, then C is the direct sum of simple submodules. Also show that if C is simple (or the direct sum of simple modules), then $NC = 0$.

3. Show that if $NC = 0$, then Hom $_R (A, C) \cong$ Hom $_{R/N}(A/NA, C)$ in a natural way.

4. Let $\cdots P_n \xrightarrow{d_n} \cdots P_0 \xrightarrow{\varepsilon} A \rightarrow 0$ be a projective resolution of A. Now form

$$\cdots P_n/NP_n \xrightarrow{d_n} \cdots \xrightarrow{\delta_1} P_0/NP_0. \tag{$*$}$$

This is no longer a projective resolution, and it need not even be exact. However, if C is such that $NC = 0$, show that $\mathrm{Ext}^n (A, C)$ can be computed as the homology groups of the Hom of (*) into C (note that the Hom is over R or R/N; it does not make any difference here):

$$0 \rightarrow \mathrm{Hom}\ (P_0/NP_0, C) \xrightarrow{\bar{\delta_1}'} \mathrm{Hom}\ (P_1/NP_1, C) \xrightarrow{\bar{\delta_2}} \cdots$$

5. Show that (*) is exact at P_1/NP_1 if and only if $\mathrm{Ext}^1 (A, S) = 0$ for all simple modules S.

6. Show that if $\mathrm{Ext}^1 (A, S) = 0$ for any simple module, then $\mathrm{Ext}^1 (A, C) = 0$ for any module C such that $NC = 0$.

7. Let $T =$ the direct sum of one each of all the simple modules. Prove that A is projective if and only if $\mathrm{Ext}^1 (A,T) = 0$.

8. Let A be a finitely generated R module; show that A has a projective resolution with finitely generated projectives.

9. Let X be a finitely generated R module and let C be a simple R module. If Δ is the endomorphism ring of C (recall that this is a division ring) make Hom (X, C) into a Δ module (that is, Δ vector space). Prove that this is a finite dimensional vector space.

10. Use Exercise 9 to show that $\mathrm{Ext}^n (A, C)$ is also a finite dimensional Δ vector space.

(4)

Various Dimensions

In this chapter we plan to introduce and study some of the homological dimensions. For the various projective dimensions, this is fairly simple, since we have already developed a considerable amount of machinery using projective modules. We also need the injective dimension, and for this it is necessary to do a little spade work in order to show that rings have enough injective modules. The reason we need to consider injective dimension is that it is necessary if we are to prove one of the fundamental theorems of this chapter: that the global dimension is the supremum of the projective dimensions of the cyclic modules.

First, we shall discuss a few preliminaries. The following theorem is useful for turning Ext^n of something into Ext^1 of something else.

The Shifting Theorem. If

$$0 \to A \to P \to B \to 0$$

is exact with P projective, then $\text{Ext}^n (A, C) = \text{Ext}^{n+1} (B, C)$ for all C and all $n \geq 1$.

Proof. The exact sequence of homology in the first variable of Ext gives

$$\cdots \to \text{Ext}^n (P, C) \to \text{Ext}^n (A, C) \xrightarrow{\theta} \text{Ext}^{n+1} (B, C) \to \text{Ext}^{n+1} (P, C) \to \cdots.$$

Since $\text{Ext}^n (P, C) = \text{Ext}^{n+1} (P, C) = (0)$, θ is an isomorphism.

COROLLARY. If $\{P_n\}$ is a projective resolution of A, then $\text{Ext}^n (A, C) = \text{Ext}^1 (\text{Im } d_{n-1}, C)$ for all C and all $n \geq 1$.

Proof. Since each of the sequences

$$0 \to \text{Im } d_1 \to P_0 \to A \to 0$$

and

$$0 \to \text{Im } d_{n+1} \to P_n \to \text{Im } d_n \to 0, \qquad n = 1, 2, \cdots,$$

is exact,

$$
\begin{aligned}
\text{Ext}^n (A, C) &= \text{Ext}^{n-1} (\text{Im } d_1, C) \\
&= \text{Ext}^{n-2} (\text{Im } d_2, C) = \cdots \\
&= \text{Ext}^1 (\text{Im } d_{n-1}, C).
\end{aligned}
$$

47

Now we come to the principal object of study in this chapter.

DEFINITION.   The *projective dimension $Pd(A)$* of an R module A is the smallest positive integer n such that $\text{Ext}^{n+1}(A, C) = 0$ for all C, if such an integer n exists. If no such n exists, then $Pd(A) = \infty$. Clearly, $Pd(A) = 0$ if and only if A is projective.

The Dimension Theorem.   The following statements are equivalent:

(1) If $\{P_k\}$ is any projective resolution of A, then $\text{Im } d_n$ is projective.

(2) A has a projective resolution

$$0 \to \bar{P}_n \to \bar{P}_{n-1} \to \cdots \to \bar{P}_0 \to A \to 0.$$

(3) $\text{Ext}^{n+j}(A, C) = (0)$ for all C and all $j \geq 1$.

(4) $\text{Ext}^{n+1}(A, C) = (0)$ for all C.

Proof. $(1) \to (2)$.   If $\{P_k\}$ is any projective resolution of A, then

$$0 \to \text{Im } d_n \to P_{n-1} \to \cdots \to A \to 0$$

is another.

$(4) \to (1)$.   Let $\{P_k\}$ be a projective resolution for A. Since

$$0 = \text{Ext}^{n+1}(A, C) = \text{Ext}^1(\text{Im } d_n, C),$$

$\text{Im } d_n$ is projective.

The implications that $(2) \to (3)$, $(3) \to (4)$ are simple.

DEFINITION.   *The left global dimension of a ring R* (l.gl.dim.R,) is

$$\sup Pd(M) | M \text{ is an } R \text{ module.}$$

Also, we consider the following finitistic dimensions:

$$LFPD(R) = \sup Pd(M) | M$$

is an R module and $Pd(M) < \infty$;

$$LfPD(R) = \sup Pd(M) | M$$

is a finitely generated R module and $Pd(M) < \infty$.

The right dimensions are defined analogously.

From the definitions, it is clear that we have the following inequalities:

$$\text{l.gl.dim.} R \geq LFPD(R) \geq LfPD(R). \qquad (4.1)$$

Also, it is clear that l.gl.dim.$R = 0$ is equivalent to R being semisimple with minimum condition (recall the theorem of Chapter 2 and the condition "every R module is projective").

Let us now turn our attention to injective modules. We shall return to consider the global dimension a little later.

Our first task is to show that every ring has "enough" injective modules. We shall prove that every R module can be embedded as a submodule of an injective R module. There does not seem to be any short elementary way to do this. The analogous theorem for projective modules (that every R module is the homomorphic image of a projective module) was fairly simple to prove because we could easily construct many free (hence projective) modules.

The program we intend to follow in constructing injectives is to first construct enough injectives for the ring of integers. Then we shall use these to construct injectives for arbitrary rings.

The following theorem and its corollary give some useful criteria for recognizing injective modules.

Injective Test Theorem. The R module Q is injective if and only if for each left ideal L of R, every homomorphism of L to Q can be extended to a homomorphism of R to Q.

Proof. Another way to phrase the condition of the theorem is that every diagram of the form

$$0 \to L \xrightarrow{\mu} R,$$
$$\downarrow$$
$$Q$$

where μ is the injection of L into R, can be embedded in a commutative diagram of the form

$$0 \to L \xrightarrow{\mu} R$$
$$\downarrow \swarrow \quad .$$
$$Q$$

Clearly then, if Q is injective, this can be done. The more difficult part of the proof is to prove that a Q with this property is injective.

Suppose now that the module Q has the above property and suppose that we have the diagram

$$0 \to X \xrightarrow{j} Y$$
$$\downarrow f$$
$$Q$$

with exact row. Let S be the collection of pairs (Y_α, f_α), where $\text{Im } j \subseteq Y_\alpha \subseteq Y$ and $f_\alpha: Y_\alpha \to Q$ has the property that $f_\alpha j = f$. Partially order S by $(Y_\alpha, f_\alpha) \geq$

(Y_β, f_β), provided $Y_\alpha \supseteq Y_\beta$ and $f_\alpha = f_\beta$ on Y_β. By Zorn's lemma, S has a maximal element (Y_0, f_0). Suppose $Y_0 \neq Y$. Let $x \in Y$, $x \notin Y_0$, and look at $L = \{r \in R | rx \in Y_0\}$. It is clear that L is a left ideal of R. Moreover, one checks to see that the equation $g(y) = f_0(yx)$ for y in L defines a homomorphism g of L into Q. By assumption this can be extended to g', a homomorphism from R into Q. Now let $g'(1) = c_0$ in Q and observe that if $rx \in Y_0$, then $f_0(rx) = g(r) = rc_0$.

Now let Y' be generated by Y_0 and x, and define f' by the equation $f'(y_0 + rx) = f_0(y_0) + rc_0$. We note that f' will be a homomorphism if it is well defined. It is sufficient to show that it is well defined "at zero"; that is, if $0 = y_0 + rx$, then $f_0(y_0) + rc_0 = 0$. Apply f_0 to $y_0 + rx$ in Y_0 and note that rx is in Y_0; then $0 = f_0(y_0) + f_0(rx) = f_0(y_0) + rc_0$, as desired.

But (Y', f') is in S and is strictly larger than (Y_0, f_0); hence we have arrived at a contradiction. Consequently, $Y = Y_0$, and we obtain the commutative diagram

$$0 \to X \xrightarrow{j} Y$$
$$f \downarrow \swarrow f_0$$
$$Q$$

Therefore, Q is injective.

COROLLARY (CYCLICS, INJECTIVES, AND EXT). The following conditions are equivalent:

(1) Q is an injective R module.
(2) $\operatorname{Ext}^n (A, Q) = 0$ for all R modules A, $n \geq 1$.
(3) $\operatorname{Ext}^1 (C, Q) = 0$ for all cyclic R modules C.

Proof. We shall prove the implications in order, starting with (1) implies (2). Let Q be injective and let A be an R module. Form the exact sequence $0 \to M \xrightarrow{j} P \xrightarrow{\pi} A \to 0$ with P projective (the beginning of a projective resolution) and plug this into the first variable of Ext $(\cdot Q)$ to get

$$\operatorname{Hom} (P, Q) \xrightarrow{j'} \operatorname{Hom} (M, Q) \xrightarrow{\theta} \operatorname{Ext}^1 (A, Q) \xrightarrow{\pi'} \operatorname{Ext}^1 (P, Q) = 0$$

exact. Since P is projective, we obtain the equality at the end. Also, j' is an epimorphism because $\operatorname{Hom} (\cdot Q)$ sends short exact sequences to short exact sequences. But then θ and π^1 are both zero maps and $\operatorname{Ext}^1 (A, Q) = 0$.

We continue the proof by completing an induction on the superscript n. Suppose that $\operatorname{Ext}^n (A, Q) = 0$ for all R modules A. Then, in the exact sequence of homology in the first variable of Ext, we see that

$$\operatorname{Ext}^n (M, Q) \to \operatorname{Ext}^{n+1} (A, Q) \to \operatorname{Ext}^{n+1} (P, Q),$$

where the first term is zero by the induction hypothesis and the last term is zero because P is projective. Thus, $\operatorname{Ext}^{n+1} (A, Q) = 0$ also.

The implication that (2) implies (3) is clear. We use the preceding theorem to show that (3) implies (1). Let L be a left ideal of R and consider the short exact sequence $0 \to L \to R \to C \to 0$, where j is the injection of L into R and where C is the cyclic module R/L. Put this into the first variable of Ext to get

$$\text{Hom } (R, Q) \overset{j'}{\to} \text{Hom } (L, Q) \to \text{Ext}^1 (C, Q) = 0$$

exact. But, since $\text{Ext}^1 (C, Q) = 0$, we see that j' is an epimorphism. This means that every homomorphism of L to Q can be extended to a homomorphism of R to Q. By the preceding theorem, we see that Q is injective. This completes the proof of the corollary.

It might be instructive to pause for a moment and examine Ext as a test for projectives and injectives. In Chapter 3 we proved that P is projective if and only if $\text{Ext}^n (P, X) = 0$ for all R modules X and all $n \geq 1$. In this chapter we have shown that a module Q is injective if and only if $\text{Ext}^n (Y, Q) = 0$ for all R modules Y, and $n \geq 1$. Thus, we have a way of using the vanishing of Ext to test for injective and projective modules.

An alert reader may have noticed that in using Ext to test for injectives, one need only to check whether $\text{Ext}^1 (C, Q) = 0$ for cyclic C (the preceding corollary). One might ask if the corresponding result (or something like it) holds for projectives. That is, if $\text{Ext}^1 (P, C) = 0$ for cyclic C, then P is projective. This is false in general. It can be shown that if R is the ring of p-adic integers and Q is its quotient field, then $\text{Ext}^1 (Q, C) = 0$ for all cyclic C, but Q is not R projective. For just what rings the vanishing of $\text{Ext}^1 (P, \cdot)$ on cyclic modules implies that P is projective is not known. It is not even known for the ring of integers. For some interesting results on these topics see Nunke [Ref. 31].

Let us now turn our attention to the ring Z of integers. In the following discussion, we shall show that Z has enough injectives.

DEFINITION. An abelian group A is called *divisible* if, for each $a \in A$ and each $n \in Z$, the equation $a = nx$ has a solution x in A (x need not be a unique solution).

There are two obvious properties of divisible groups that we shall need:

(1) A direct sum of divisible groups is a divisible group.
(2) A homomorphic image of a divisible group is again a divisible group.

THEOREM. A is divisible if and only if A is Z-injective.

Proof. Suppose that A is divisible and f is a homomorphism from an ideal I of Z into A. Recall that the ideals in the ring of integers are principal, that is, $I = (n)$ and $f(n) = a$ in A. Then the equation $yn = a$ can be solved for y in A, and by defining $f'(1) = y$, we see that we have an extension of f to all of Z. Thus, by one of our tests for injectives, A is injective.

Conversely, suppose that A is injective. Let $a \in A$ and $0 \neq n \in Z$, and define the homomorphism f from $(n) \subseteq Z$ to A by $f(n) = a$. Extend this to f' on all of Z, using the fact that A is injective. Then $f'(1)$ is a solution in A to the equation $ny = a$. Therefore, A is divisible.

We are now in a position to embed every Z module (abelian group) in an injective Z module (divisible abelian group).

THEOREM.   Every abelian group can be embedded in a divisible group.

Proof. We use the fact that the group Q of rationals is divisible.

Let j be the injection map so that $0 \to Z \to Q$ is exact. Thus, free groups (being direct sums of copies of Z) can be embedded in divisible groups. (Recall that the direct sum of copies of Q is divisible.)

Now let A be any group and let F be a free group mapping onto A with kernel K:

$$0 \to K \to F \to A \to 0 \qquad \text{exact.}$$

Now embed F in a divisible group D. But $A \cong F/K$, which is a submodule of D/K, and the latter is divisible because D is. Thus we have embedded A in a divisible group.

Let R be a ring and let C be an R module. If Q is a Z module, then there is a useful way of turning $\text{Hom}_Z (C, Q)$ into a *right* R module. For $f \in \text{Hom}_Z (C, Q)$, $c \in C$, $r \in R$, we define $fr(c) = f(rc)$; it is easy to check that this makes $\text{Hom}_Z (C, Q)$ into a right R module. Similarly, if we start out with a right R module A, then we can make $\text{Hom}_Z (A, Q)$ into an R module by defining $rf(a) = f(ar)$ for $f \in \text{Hom}_Z (A, Q) r \in R$ and $a \in A$.

If we have R modules A and B and an R homomorphism $\theta: A \to B$, then this induces an R homomorphism $\text{Hom}_Z (B, Q) \xrightarrow{\theta} \text{Hom}_Z (A, Q)$ defined by $\theta'(f) = f\theta$. Also, if $Q \to T$ is a Z homomorphism, this induces an R homomorphism $\text{Hom}_Z (A, Q) \to \text{Hom}_Z (A, T)$, the usual induced map in the second variable.

One of the reasons for introducing the R module $\text{Hom}_Z (A, Q)$ becomes clear from the following lemma.

Injective Producing Lemma. If Q is Z-injective, then the R module $\text{Hom}_Z (R, Q)$ is R-injective.

Proof. To test for the R injectivity of $\text{Hom}_Z (R, Q)$, it is enough, from our previous results on injectives, to examine the diagram

$$0 \to L \xrightarrow{j} R$$
$$\downarrow f$$
$$\text{Hom}_Z(R, Q),$$

where L is left ideal of R and j is the injection of L into R. For x in L, $f(x)$ is a Z homomorphism of R to Q, so $f(x)$ applied to y in R is an element of Q.

That is, we can think of f as a function of two variables $x \in L$ and $y \in R$ with values $f(x, y)$ in Q. We see that if we think of f in this way, then f must satisfy the following conditions:

$$f(x, y + y') = f(x, y) + f(x, y'), \tag{4.2}$$
$$f(x + x', y) = f(x, y) + f(x', y), \tag{4.3}$$
$$f(rx, y) = f(x, yr), \tag{4.4}$$

for the x's in L and y's and r in R.

Condition (4.2) expresses the fact that for fixed x, $f(x)$ is a Z homomorphism of R to Q. Conditions (4.3) and (4.4) follow from the fact that f is an R homomorphism of L to $\mathrm{Hom}_Z (R, Q)$, from the way the elements of $\mathrm{Hom}_Z (R, Q)$ add and the way R acts on $\mathrm{Hom}_Z (R, Q)$.

Now consider the function g defined by $g(x) = f(x, 1)$ for x in L. This is a Z homomorphism of L into Q, and since Q is Z-injective, we can extend g to a Z homomorphism g' from R to Q. We use g' to construct an extension of our original homomorphism f to all of R.

For x, y in R, define $f'(x, y) = g'(yx)$ and check to see that the following conditions hold for x's and y's in R:

$$f'(x + x', y) = f'(x, y) + f'(x', y), \tag{4.2'}$$
$$f'(x, y + y') = f'(x, y) + f'(x, y'), \tag{4.3'}$$
$$f'(rx, y) = f'(x, yr) \qquad \text{for } r \text{ in } R, \tag{4.4'}$$
$$\text{and} \qquad f(x, y) = f(yx, 1) = g(yx) \qquad \text{for } x \text{ in } L \text{ and } y \text{ in } R.$$
$$= f'(x, y) \tag{4.5}$$

Thus f' can be considered as an R homomorphism of R to $\mathrm{Hom}_Z (R, C)$, and by property (4.5), f' is an extension of f. The above proof shows that $\mathrm{Hom}_Z (R, Q)$ is R-injective.

In the following theorem, we shall show that the construction of injectives given by the preceding lemma provides enough injectives so that every R module can be embedded as a submodule of an injective R module.

THEOREM (Enough Injectives). If A is an R module, there exists an injective R module of the form $\mathrm{Hom}_Z (R, Q)$, where Q is an injective Z module such that the sequence

$$0 \to A \to \mathrm{Hom}_Z (R, Q)$$

is exact as a sequence of R modules.

Proof. Think of A as merely an abelian group, and using the fact that there are enough Z injectives, embed A into a Z-injective Q:

$$0 \to A \xrightarrow{j} Q.$$

This induces an exact sequence

$$0 \to \mathrm{Hom}_Z (R, A) \xrightarrow{j'} \mathrm{Hom}_Z (R, Q),$$

where this is an exact sequence of R modules. By the lemma, we know that $\text{Hom}_Z(R, Q)$ is an injective R module and that the R module $\text{Hom}_Z(R, A)$ is isomorphic to an R submodule of it.

The R module $\text{Hom}_R(R, A)$ is R-isomorphic to an R submodule of $\text{Hom}_Z(R, A)$, for, after all, R homomorphisms are Z homomorphisms. Finally, we see that the R module $\text{Hom}_R(R, A)$ is R-isomorphic to A itself under the mapping that sends the homomorphism f to $f(1)$ in A.

Tracing back through all the injections, we see that we can embed A as a submodule of $\text{Hom}_Z(R, Q)$.

We turn now to the injective dimension of an R module. Observe the similarity of this discussion with that of projective dimension.

DEFINITION. An exact sequence of R modules,

$$0 \to C \to Q_0 \to Q_1 \to \cdots,$$

where each Q_i is injective, is called an *injective resolution of C*.

The enough injectives theorem implies that every R module has an injective resolution.

Shifting Theorem for Injectives. If

$$0 \to C \to Q \to D \to 0$$

is exact, with Q injective, then

$$\text{Ext}^n(A, D) = \text{Ext}^{n+1}(A, C), \qquad n \geq 1.$$

Proof. Apply the exact sequence of homology theorem in the second variable of Ext to the given exact sequence and use the cyclics injectives and Ext corollary.

COROLLARY. If

$$0 \to M \to Q_0 \xrightarrow{d_0} Q_1 \cdots$$

is an injective resolution of M, then for any A,

$$\begin{aligned}
\text{Ext}^{n+1}(A, M) &= \text{Ext}^n(A, \text{Im } d_0) \\
&= \text{Ext}^{n-1}(A, \text{Im } d_1) = \cdots \\
&= \text{Ext}^1(A, \text{Im } d_{n-1}).
\end{aligned}$$

Proof. The proof is a repeated application of the shifting theorem for injectives.

The injective dimension is now defined in very close analogy to the projective dimension.

DEFINITION. The *injective dimension* Id (C) of an R module C is the greatest positive integer n such that $\operatorname{Ext}^n (A, C) \neq 0$ for some module A. If no such n exists, we say Id $(C) = \infty$.

The Injective Dimension Theorem. The following statements are equivalent:

(1) If Q_k is any injective resolution of C, then Im d_{n-1} is injective.
(2) C has an injective resolution $0 \to C \to Q_1 \to \cdots \to Q_n \to 0 \to \cdots$.
(3) $\operatorname{Ext}^{n+j} (A, C) = 0$ for all $j \geq 1$ and all A.
(4) $\operatorname{Ext}^{n+1} (A, C) = 0$ for all A.
(5) $\operatorname{Ext}^{n+1} (A, C) = 0$ for all cyclic A.

Proof. (1) implies (2) is easy because we can stop the injective resolution at Im d_{n-1} and continue with zeros from there on. (2) implies (3) follows from the preceding corollary. The implications that (3) implies (4) implies (5) are obvious.

Finally, (5) implies (1) follows from the cyclics injectives and Ext corollary.

Perhaps we should comment here on an alternate method for producing Ext. If

$$0 \to D \to Q_0 \to Q_1 \to \cdots$$

is an injective resolution of D, then one can form the complex

$$C: 0 \to \operatorname{Hom} (A, Q_0) \to \operatorname{Hom} (A, Q_1) \to \cdots$$

and compute the homology groups of this complex. It is not hard to show that each homology group $H_n(C)$ is isomorphic to $\operatorname{Ext}^n (A, D)$. In fact, this can be taken as the definition of $\operatorname{Ext}^n (A, D)$, and the whole program for Ext can be worked out from this definition. We shall not do that because we have already established most of the basic properties that we need.

Let us now return to the global dimension. Following is a fundamental theorem on global dimension.

Global Dimension Theorem.

$$\text{l.gl.dim.} R = \sup Pd(A)|A \qquad \text{a cyclic } R \text{ module}$$

Proof. Suppose that $\sup Pd(A)|A$ cyclic $= n$. Then, for every module C, $\operatorname{Ext}^{n+1} (A, C) = 0$ for all cyclic A by the dimension theorem. But then the injective dimension theorem implies that $Ext^{n+1}(A, C) = 0$ for *all* A and for *all* C. Applying the dimension theorem again, we see that $Pd(A) \leq n$ for all modules A and l.gl.dim.$R \leq n$. It follows that l.gl.dim.$R = n$.

Of course the analogous theorem holds for right modules and the right global dimension. Later on we shall look into conditions that show the left and right global dimensions to be equal. Kaplansky has shown that they are not, in general, equal [Ref. 23].

Notice that this theorem states that if the global dimension is finite, the set of inequalities (4.1) on the various finitistic dimensions turns into a set of equalities. This tells us what the finitistic dimensions are in that case. However, if l.gl.dim. $(R) = \infty$, the theorem does not help us with the finistic dimensions at all.

COROLLARY.   If l.gl.dim.$R \geq 1$, then

$$\text{l.gl.dim. } R = [\sup Pd(L) | L \text{ is a left ideal}] + 1.$$

Proof. Since l.gl.dim.$R \geq 1$, there is a cyclic R module C with $Pd(C) \neq 0$. C is an R-homomorphic image of R. Let L be the kernel of this R homomorphism (L is a left ideal) and look at $0 \rightarrow L \rightarrow R \rightarrow C \rightarrow 0$. Since R is free, $Pd(L) + 1 = Pd(C)$.

THEOREM.   If R has a composition series of left ideals, then

$$\text{l.gl.dim. } R = \sup \dot{P}d(S) | S \text{ is a simple } R \text{ module.}$$

Proof. Since simple R modules are cyclic, it suffices to consider the case where the right side is equal to $n < \infty$. We shall show that every R module M possessing a composition series has projective dimension less than or equal to n. Since every cyclic R module (being an R-homomorphic image of R) has a composition series, the global dimension theorem implies the result. We induce on the length r of composition series.

If M is an R module having a composition series of length 1, $Pd(M) \leq n$, since M is simple. Assume that the theorem holds for all R modules having a composition series of length less than r. Let M be an R module with a composition series of length r, say, the series $M \supset M_1 \cdots M_r = (0)$. Then, setting $S = M/M_1$,

$$0 \rightarrow M_1 \rightarrow M \rightarrow S \rightarrow 0$$

is exact and S is simple. This induces the exact sequence

$$Ext^{n+1}(S, C) \rightarrow Ext^{n+1}(M, C) \rightarrow Ext^{n+1}(M_1, C)$$

and by the inductive hypothesis (since S and M_1 have composition series of length less than r),

$$0 \to \mathrm{Ext}^{n+1} (M, C) \to 0 \qquad \text{exact for all } C.$$

That is, $Pd(M) \leq n$.

COROLLARY. If R has a composition series of left ideals and if l.gl.dim.R $\neq 0$, then

l.gl.dim.$R = [\sup Pd(L)|L$ is a maximal left ideal in $R] + 1$.

Proof. If S is simple, there is a maximal left ideal L such that

$$0 \to L \to R \to S \to 0$$

is exact. Hence, $Pd(L) + 1 = Pd(S)$.

The following theorem holds over any ring.

THEOREM. If

$$0 \to A \to B \to C \to 0$$

is exact, then if any two of the R modules have finite projective dimension, so does the third.

Proof. Consider the exact sequence of homology in the first variable of Ext with arbitrary D:

$$\mathrm{Ext}^{n-1} (A, D) \to \mathrm{Ext}^n (C, D) \to \mathrm{Ext}^n (B, D) \to \mathrm{Ext}^n (A, D)$$
$$\to \mathrm{Ext}^{n+1} (C, D) \to \cdots.$$

If n is large enough, the Ext's of the finite dimensional modules will be zero, and therefore the Ext of the other must also be zero.

Let us now turn our attention to comparing the left and right global dimensions. In the following discussion, we shall show that for a large class of rings (Noetherian rings), the left and right global dimensions are equal. First, we need a definition.

DEFINITION. An R module A is called *Noetherian* if every R submodule is finitely generated.

It is quite easy to show that the condition that every R submodule be finitely generated is equivalent to the ascending chain condition on R submodules (ACC). Also, R submodules and R-factor modules of Noetherian modules are Noetherian.

Lemma. If A and C are Noetherian, and if

$$0 \to A \xrightarrow{j} B \xrightarrow{\pi} C \to 0$$

is exact, then B is Noetherian.

Proof. Let B' be a submodule of B; then $\pi(B')$ is a submodule of C and has generators $x_1 \cdots x_n$. Choose $y_1 \cdots y_n \in B'$ so that $\pi(y_i) = x_i$. Now form the intersection of B' with Im j, and this is finitely generated by $z_1 \cdots z_r$. Now we claim that the set $y_1 \cdots y_n z_1 \cdots z_r$ generates B'. We show this as follows: Let $b \in B'$, $\pi(b) \in \pi(B')$, so

$$\pi(b) = \sum^{m} r_i x_i.$$

But then

$$\pi\left(b - \sum^{n} r_i y_i\right) = 0 \quad \text{and} \quad b - \sum^{n} r_i y_i \in B' \cap \text{Im } j.$$

That is,

$$b - \sum^{n} r_i y_i = \sum^{r} \tau_j z_j \quad \text{and} \quad b = \sum^{n} r_i y_i + \sum^{r} \tau_j z_j.$$

DEFINITION. A ring R is *left (right) Noetherian*, provided it is Noetherian when considered as a left (right) module over itself.

THEOREM. A finitely generated module over a left Noetherian ring R is Noetherian.

Proof. Induce on the number n of generators. For $n = 1$, $A = R/L$ and is Noetherian. Assume the theorem for modules over less than n elements and let M be generated by $x_1, \cdots, x_n$. Let M_0 be generated by $x_1, \cdots, x_{n-1}$ and form

$$0 \to M_0 \to M \to M/M_0 \to 0.$$

Since M_0 and M/M_0 are on $n - 1$ and 1 generator, respectively, the preceding lemma shows that M is Noetherian.

The following theorem is the best known one for comparing the left and right global dimensions.

THEOREM. If R is left and right Noetherian, then the left and right global dimensions are equal.

Proof. We shall now sketch a proof that is complete except for one sticky point. Later, in a lemma, we shall explain how to get past this point.

The idea of the proof is to show that the right global dimension is always greater than or equal to the left. Then the same argument, with left and right reversed, gives the theorem.

Let B be a cyclic R module; then B has a projective resolution,

$$\cdots F_n \to F_{n-1} \to \cdots \to F_0 \to B \to 0, \tag{4.6}$$

where each F_i is a finitely generated, free R module. This is where we need the fact that the ring is left Noetherian. Now let Q be an injective Z module, and form the induced sequence of *right* modules:

$$0 \to \operatorname{Hom}_Z (B, Q) \to \operatorname{Hom}_Z (F_0, Q) \to \cdots . \tag{4.7}$$

The claim is that this is always an *injective* resolution of the *right* module $\operatorname{Hom}_Z (B, Q)$. Since each F_i is the direct sum of a finite number of copies of the ring R, and each $\operatorname{Hom}_Z (R, Q)$ is injective (the injective producing lemma), it follows that each $\operatorname{Hom}_Z (F_i, Q)$ is R-injective.

We know that $\operatorname{Hom}_Z (\cdot Q)$ is an exact functor because Q is injective. That is, $\operatorname{Hom}_Z (\cdot Q)$ when applied to short exact sequences gives short exact sequences. The long exact sequence (4.6) can be thought of as a collection of short exact sequences,

$$0 \to \operatorname{Im} \delta_1 \to F_0 \to B \to 0,$$

$$0 \to \operatorname{Im} \delta_{i+1} \to F_i \to \operatorname{Im} \delta_i \to 0, \qquad i \geq 1,$$

all pasted together at each $\operatorname{Im} \delta_i$. Apply $\operatorname{Hom}_Z (\cdot Q)$ separately to each of these short sequences and then paste the resulting sequences back together. We claim that this implies that the sequence (4.7) is exact.

If $Pd(B) \geq n$, then $\operatorname{Im} \delta_n$ is not projective (the dimension theorem). If only we could claim that this implies that $\operatorname{Hom}_Z (\operatorname{Im} \delta_n, Q)$ is not R-injective for a suitable Z-injective, Q then we should know from the sequence (4.7) that $\operatorname{Id}(\operatorname{Hom}_Z (B, Q) \geq n$. This is the sticky point. We shall establish later that if X is a finitely generated, *non*projective R module, then there exists an injective Z module Q such that $\operatorname{Hom}_Z (X, Q)$ is *not* R-injective.

Let us, for the moment, grant the sticky point. The above argument says that for some Z module Q there exists a right R module A such that $\operatorname{Ext}^n (A, \operatorname{Hom}_Z (B, Q)) \neq 0$. That is, for the cyclic module B with $Pd(B) \geq n$, there exists a right module A such that $Pd(A) \geq n$. Hence, the right global dimension of R is greater than or equal to $\sup Pd(B)|B$ cyclic. By the global dimension theorem, the latter is the left global dimensional. This completes the proof of the theorem, with the exception of the sticky point.

We embark on a proof of the sticky point via some lemmas. The first lemma holds without any finiteness conditions on the rings or modules.

Lemma 1. If K is an R submodule of F, a free R module, and if $\operatorname{Hom}_Z (F/K, Q)$ is R-injective for all injective Z modules Q, then for each right ideal H of R,

$$HF \cap K = HK.$$

Proof. Note that forming HF and HK, where H is a right ideal and F, K are left modules, is something we do not usually do. However, these are subgroups of F, and we have in general that $HF \cap K \supseteq HK$. Let us suppose that $HF \cap K$ contains HK properly. Thus, there exists an element $af \in K$ for $a \in H$, $f \in F$ such that $af \notin HK$. There is a Z-injective Q and a Z homomorphism $\mu: K \to Q$ such that $\mu(af) \neq 0$, but $\mu(HK) = 0$. (For instance, let μ be the embedding of K/HK in a Z-injective Q.)

Suppose also that $\text{Hom}_Z (F/K, Q)$ is injective; use this to split the sequence

$$0 \to \text{Hom}_Z (F/K, Q) \to \text{Hom}_Z (F, Q) \underset{\rho}{\overset{j'}{\underset{\leftarrow}{\rightarrow}}} \text{Hom}_Z (K, Q) \to 0,$$

which is induced by

$$0 \to K \overset{j}{\to} F \to F/K \to 0,$$

where j is the injection of K into F.

We apply the splitting ρ to the element $\mu a \in \text{Hom}_Z (K, Q)$, where μ, a are as chosen above. First we note that $\mu a(k) = 0$ for all $k \in K$ because $\mu(HK) = 0$ and $a \in H$. Thus, it follows that $\mu a = 0$ and $\rho(\mu a) = 0$.

However, form $(\rho\mu)a \in \text{Hom}_Z (F, Q)$ and apply it to f as chosen above. It follows that $(\rho\mu)a\{f\} = \rho\mu(af)$ and $af \in K$. Thus, $j'\rho\mu(af) = \mu(af) \neq 0$, so it follows that $j'[(\rho\mu)a] \neq 0$, and hence $(\rho\mu)a \neq 0$. But then $(\rho\mu)a \neq \rho(\mu a)$ and we have arrived at a contradiction.

The modules F/K of the preceding lemma satisfying the condition $\text{Hom}_Z (F/K, Q)$ injective for all Z injectives Q are called *flat* modules. These modules are usually studied by use of another functor, which we have not developed here. Since Lemma 1 also has a true converse (a fact that we do not need or prove), the flatness of F/K is also characterized by the condition $HF \cap K = HK$ holding for all right ideals H.

Lemma 2. If $K \subseteq F$ free, with K finitely generated and such that $HF \cap K = HK$ for all right ideals H of R, then the sequence $0 \to K \to F \to F/K \to 0$ splits and F/K is projective.

Proof. The idea of the proof is to construct a homomorphism $\phi: F \to K$ with the property that $\phi|K = $ identity. This can be done in the following manner: Let $u_1 \cdots u_r$ be a set of elements in K. We shall show by induction on r that there is a homomorphism $\phi: F \to K$ such that $\phi(u_i) = u_i$ for $i = 1 \cdots r$. Since K is finitely generated, we eventually get the desired homomorphism.

We leave it to the reader to check to see that $F \cong K \oplus \text{Ker } \phi$ where $\phi: F \to K$ and $\phi|K = $ identity. So, we proceed with the induction.

Let $u \in K$, and represent u in terms of a basis x_α of F, $u = r_1 x_{\alpha_1} + \cdots + r_n x_{d_n}$. Form the right ideal $H = \sum r_i R$ generated by $r_1 \cdots r_n$. Note that the element $u \in HF \cap K$; so, by our hypothesis, $u \in HK$ and thus $u = r_1 k_1 + \cdots + r_n k_n$, where the r_i are as above and the $k_1 \cdots k_n$ are suitable elements of K. On the basis elements $x_{\alpha_1} \cdots x_{\alpha_n}$, let $\phi(x_{\alpha_i}) = k_i$; for other basis elements x_β, let $\phi(x_\beta) = 0$. This defines the homomorphism $\phi: F \to K$, and we observe that $\phi(u) = u$.

Now, for the general case, let $u_1 \cdots u_n$ be a set of n elements of K, and suppose that the problem of constructing the desired homomorphisms can be solved for sets of fewer than n elements. By the proof for one element, we find $\phi_n: F \to K$ such that $\phi_n(u_n) = u_n$. Now let $v_i = u_i - \phi_n(u_i)$ for $i = 1 \cdots n - 1$. By the induction hypothesis, there exists $\phi': F \to K$ such that $\phi'(v_i) = v_i$ for $i = 1 \cdots n - 1$. Let $\phi = \phi' + \phi_n - \phi'\phi_n$, and check to see that this does the job:

$$\phi(u_n) = \phi'(u_n) + \phi_n(u_n) - \phi'(\phi_n(u_n)) = \phi_n(u_n) = u_n,$$
$$\phi(u_i) = \phi'(u_i) + \phi_n(u_i) - \phi'\phi_n(u_i) = \phi'[u_i - \phi_n(u_i)] + \phi_n(u_i)$$
$$= u_i \quad \text{for } i \leq i \leq n - 1.$$

This completes the proof of the lemma.

In Lemma 2, the module F/K, with F free and K finitely generated, is called *finitely related*. Noetherian rings are characterized by the condition that finitely generated modules are finitely related. Lemma 2 can be rephrased as, "Finitely related flat modules are projective." Note that in the proof of the lemma we did not require that F be finitely generated, but only K. So, the lemma holds in a slightly more general context than finitely generated modules over Noetherian rings.

But let us now return to those rings to clear up the sticky point that started us on this series of lemmas.

Lemma 3 (*The Sticky Point*). Let A be a finitely generated module over a (left) Noetherian ring. If $\mathrm{Hom}_Z(A, Q)$ is injective for all Z-injectives Q, then A is projective.

Proof. Form the exact sequence $0 \to K \to F \to A \to 0$, with F free and K finitely generated. By Lemma 1, $HF \cap K = HK$ for all right ideals H. Therefore, by Lemma 2, $F \cong A \oplus K$, and A is projective.

This may be a good time to examine some examples:

(1) If R is a principal ideal domain, it is clear that every ideal is iso-morphic as a module to R itself; therefore ideals are projective. Consequently, l.gl.dim.$R = 0$ or 1, by the corollary to the global dimension theorem. Actually, it is not hard to see that principal ideal domains of global dimension 0 are fields (they must be semisimple and lack nontrivial idempotents). We see that some examples of rings of global dimension 1 are Z and $K[x]$, the polynomial ring with coefficients in a field K.

(2) It can be shown, although we shall not do it, that $K[x_1 \cdots x_n]$, the polynomial ring in n variables, with coefficients in a field K has global dimension n. In the problems at the end of this chapter we shall give other examples of rings of global dimension n.

(3) Let K be a field, and consider the ring $R = K[x]/(x^2)$, the polynomial ring factored by the ideal generated by x^2. We mention the following facts about R:

 (a) $R \supset N \supset (0)$ is a composition series for R whose N is the radical and R/N is simple.
 (b) Every projective R module has even vector space dimension over K (actually, projectives are free and direct sums of copies of R).
 (c) The simple R module R/N has a projective resolution $\{P_n\}$ such that Im δ_n has odd vector space dimension over K for all n. Hence, $Pd(R/N) = \infty$.
 (d) R has no modules of finite nonzero projective dimension; therefore, $LfPD(A) = 0$. It can be shown that $LFPD(A) = 0$ also.

(4) If l.gl.dim. $R = n$, l.gl.dim. $T = \infty$ and $LfPD(T) \leq n$, then the ring direct sum $R + T$ has the following properties:

$$l.gl.dim. \ (R + T) = \infty,$$
$$LfPD(R + T) = n.$$

Thus, by the examples of (2) and (3), we can concoct rings of infinite global dimension but arbitrary (finite) finitistic dimension.

There are a number of unsolved problems connected with finitistic dimensions. Here are some conjectures:

(1) The finitistic dimensions are finite for some large class of rings. For instance, these classes are listed in increasing order of generality (see Exercise 9 of this chapter): algebras of finite vector-space dimension over a field, rings with minimum condition on left ideals, and left Noetherian rings. Some sort of finiteness condition is required because

$$R = \prod_1^\infty R_i,$$

the product of an infinite number of rings R_i of global dimension i, has infinite finitistic dimension.

(2) It is conjectured that $LFPD(R) = LfPD(R)$ for some large class of rings also.

(3) In this chapter we showed the left and right global dimensions equal for left and right Noetherian rings. The left and right finitistic dimensions need *not* be equal as shown in [Ref. 23]. One wonders what relationships there are among them.

(4) For left and right Noetherian rings, R, finiteness of the small finitistic dimension implies that if M is a finitely generated R module, then $M \neq 0$ implies that $\mathrm{Ext}^n (M, R) \neq 0$ for some n. Is the converse true?

We shall examine $\mathrm{Ext}^n (M, R)$ in detail in the next chapter. Also we shall give some information about left and right Noetherian rings of small finitistic dimension.

(5) This is not a conjecture but a suggestion. Find some reasonable structure theorem for rings of global dimension n, assuming those finiteness conditions (for example, minimum condition on something) that are needed. Do not expect a theory as complete as the one we developed for rings of global dimension 0. Start with $n = 1$ and work up.

EXERCISES

1. Let R have minimum condition on left ideals and let T be the direct sum of one each of the simple R modules (see Exercise 7, Chapter 3). Prove $Pd(A) < n$ if and only if $\mathrm{Ext}^n (A, T) = 0$. That is, T is a test module for projective dimension.

2. Use the same assumptions as those in Exercise 1. Prove: $Id(A) < n$ if and only if $\mathrm{Ext}^n (T, A) = 0$. T is also a test module for injective dimension.

3. Prove that if $0 \rightarrow G \rightarrow Q \rightarrow B \rightarrow 0$ is exact, with Q injective, then the induced sequence in homology,

$$\mathrm{Hom}\,(A, Q) \rightarrow \mathrm{Hom}\,(A, B) \rightarrow \mathrm{Ext}^1 (A, C) \rightarrow 0,$$

is exact.

4. Prove that if $0 \rightarrow C \rightarrow Q_0 \rightarrow Q_1 \rightarrow \cdots$ is an injective resolution of C, then the complex

$$G: 0 \rightarrow \mathrm{Hom}\,(A, Q_0) \rightarrow \mathrm{Hom}\,(A, Q_1) \rightarrow \cdots$$

has homology groups $H_n(G) = \mathrm{Ext}^n (A, C)$. HINT. Ext^0 is easy; use Exercise 3 for Ext^1. Then use the shifting theorem for injectives for Ext^n.

5. Let A be a vector space over a field K with a basis $e_1 \cdots e_{n+1}, m_1 \cdots m_n$. Define the following multiplication in A:

$$e_i e_j = \delta_{ij} e_i \qquad e_i m_i e_{i+1} = m_i \qquad m_i m_j = 0.$$

Show that this is enough to extend the multiplication to all of A and that, with it, A becomes an algebra with identity $1 = e_1 + \cdots + e_{n+1}$.

6. In the algebra A defined in Exercise 5, show that

(a) The radical N of A is the subspace generated by $m_1 \cdots m_n$.

(b) A/N is the direct sum of fields isomorphic to K.

(c) A and A/N have $n + 1$ simple modules, Ae_i/Ne_i, $i = 1 \cdots n + 1$.

7. Continuing with the algebra A, show that the following is an exact sequence of A modules:

$$0 \to Re_1 \to Re_2 \to \cdots Re_i \xrightarrow{\delta} Re_{i+1} \to \cdots Re_{n+1} \to Re_{n+1}/Ne_{n+1} \to 0$$

where $\delta(e_i) = e_i m_i \in Re_{i+1}$.

8. Now deduce for the algebra A:

$$Pd\,(Re_i/Ne_i) = i - 1, \qquad i = 1 \cdots n + 1.$$

HINT. Segments of the above exact sequence are projective resolutions of each Re_i/Ne_i.

Finally, conclude l.gl.dim. $A = n$.

9. Prove that a ring with minimum condition on left ideals is left Noetherian.

10. In Exercise 9, Chapter 3, we defined Δ to be the endomorphism ring of a simple R module C. Now define $c_n(A) = [\text{Ext}^n\,(A, C): \Delta]$ the dimension of $\text{Ext}^n\,(A, C)$ over Δ. The number $c_n(A)$ is called the nth C *Betti number of* A. Show that $Pd(A) = n$ implies that $c_m(A) = 0$ for $m \geq n + 1$.

11. Let $0 \to A \to B \to D \to 0$ he an exact sequence of finitely generated R modules of finite projective dimension. Form the sum

$$\Omega(A) = \sum_{n=1}^{\infty} (-1)^n c_n(A).$$

This is really only a finite sum. Define $\Omega(B)$ and $\Omega(D)$ analogously, and prove $\Omega(B) = \Omega(A) + \Omega(D)$.

12. Again consider the exact sequence $0 \to A \to B \to D \to 0$ of finitely generated R modules, but do not assume now that they all have finite projective dimension. Prove that if any two of the three infinite sequences $c_n(A)$, $c_n(B)$, and $c_n(D)$ are bounded, then so is the third.

(5)

Duality and Quasi-Frobenius Rings

In this chapter we shall use some of our previously developed theory to establish certain facts concerning duality. Our investigation culminates with a survey of some of the properties of quasi-Frobenius rings.

In a sense, we have completed a cycle. We started the book by a structure theorem for rings, satisfying certain homological conditions. Then we developed lots of homological machinery, and now we return to the rings themselves, using the machinery that we developed.

DEFINITION. Let M be an R module. The *dual of M, M**, is the R right module $\operatorname{Hom}_R (M, R)$, where module multiplication is given by the rule

$$(fr)(x) = (f(x))r, \quad f \in M^*, \quad r \in R, \quad x \in M.$$

If M is an R right module, then the dual of M is an R module, where module multiplication is defined by

$$(rf)(x) = r(f(x)), \quad f \in M^*, \quad r \in R, \quad x \in M.$$

Once we have the dual M^* of a module M, we may form the *double dual* $M^{**} = (M^*)^*$ of M. If M is an R module (R right module), then so is its double dual. There is a natural R homomorphism of M into M^{**},

$$\sigma \colon M \to M^{**},$$

defined by the rule

$$\sigma(m)\{f^*\} = f^*(m),$$

where $m \in M, f^* \in M^*$.

We say that M is *torsionless* if σ is an R monomorphism, and that it is *reflexive* if σ is an R isomorphism. Im σ is called the *torsionless factor of M*.

EXAMPLES

1. If $M = Z/(m)$, Z the integers, then $M^* = M^{**} = (0)$.

2. Finitely generated vector spaces are reflexive (a dimension argument).

3. An arbitrary vector space is always torsionless, but not necessarily reflexive.

4. Torsionless abelian groups are torsion free, but the converse need not be true (for example, the rational numbers considered as an abelian group).

If we have the diagram $A \xrightarrow{f} B$, then this induces

$$\text{Hom}_R (B, R) \xrightarrow{f'} \text{Hom}_R (A, R)$$

or, conforming with the notation we have introduced in this chapter, $B^* \xrightarrow{f^*} A^*$. The reader may check that f^* is a module homomorphism. The reader may also check to see that the following diagram is commutative:

$$
\begin{array}{ccc}
A & \xrightarrow{\ f\ } & B \\
\sigma \downarrow & & \downarrow \sigma \\
A^{**} & \xrightarrow{f^{**}} & B^{**},
\end{array}
$$

where $f^{**} = (f^*)^*$.

Properties of (*)

(A) We already know that if $0 \to A \to B \to C \to 0$ is split exact, then so is $0 \to C^* \to B^* \to A^* \to 0$.

(B) We shall denote the R module R by $_R R$ and the R right module R by R_R. Then

$$(_R R)^* = R_R$$

and

$$(R_R)^* = {}_R R.$$

These mappings are given by $f \to f(1)$. The fact that these are R isomorphisms is easily verified.

(C) $(_R R)^{**} = {}_R R$. That the modules are R-isomorphic follows by two applications of property (B). That the R isomorphism so obtained is in fact σ is left to the reader to prove.

THEOREM.   If P is a finitely generated, projective, R module (R right module), then

(1) P^* is a finitely generated, projective, R right module (R module, respectively), and

(2) P is reflexive.

Proof.   The theorem is true for free modules F with a finite basis by the properties (A), (B), and (C) above and by induction on the number of generators. Then, a finitely generated, projective P is the image of some such free F, giving $0 \to Q \to F \to P \to 0$ split exact. By property (A), $0 \to P^* \to F^* \to Q^* \to 0$ is also split exact. This gives the commutative diagram

$$0 \rightarrow Q \quad \rightarrow F \quad \rightarrow P \quad \rightarrow 0$$
$$\sigma \downarrow \qquad \downarrow \sigma \qquad \downarrow \sigma$$
$$0 \rightarrow Q^{**} \rightarrow F^{**} \rightarrow P^{**} \rightarrow 0,$$

which has split exact rows and where the middle σ is an isomorphism. It follows that P is reflexive. This completes the proof of the theorem.

Remark. The assumption in the above theorem that P be finitely generated is necessary. It can be shown that if V is an infinite, dimensional, vector space over a field (that is, a nonfinitely generated projective over the field), then the dimensions of V^* and V^{**} are strictly larger cardinals than the dimension of V. Thus, in this case, $\sigma: V \rightarrow V^{**}$ cannot be an isomorphism.

It has been shown that

$$\oplus \sum_{1}^{\infty} Z,$$

the direct sum of a countable number of copies of the integers is reflexive. Whether this is true for *all* free modules over the integers is equivalent to an unsolved problem concerning cardinal numbers. Also, it is not hard to show that

$$\left(\oplus \sum_{1}^{\infty} Z \right)^* = \prod_{1}^{\infty} Z$$

which is *not* projective.

Third Dual Theorem. The sequence

$$0 \rightarrow A^* \xrightarrow{\tau} A^{***}$$

is exact and splits, where τ is the map of A^* into *its* second dual.

Proof. Let $\sigma: A \rightarrow A^{**}$ be the natural map of A into its second dual and consider $\sigma^* \tau$, where σ^* is the induced map $A^{***} \rightarrow A^*$. For a^* in A^*, form $\sigma^* \tau(a^*)$ and apply it to an element a in A. This is the same thing as $\tau(a^*)$ applied to $\sigma(a)$; this, in turn, is a^* applied to a. That is, $\sigma^* \tau(a^*) = a^*$ for all a^* in A^*. Hence, $\sigma^* \tau$ is identity on A^* and the theorem follows.

COROLLARY. Duals are torsionless; that is, A^* is torsionless.

Some Properties of Torsionless Modules.

(A) If $A \xrightarrow{\sigma} A^{**}$, then $\operatorname{Ker} \sigma = \bigcap_{a^* \in A^*} (\operatorname{Ker} a^*)$.

Proof. Calculate, using the definition of σ:

(B) A is torsionless if and only if $\bigcap_{a^* \in A^*} \operatorname{Ker} a^* = (0)$.

Proof.   Immediate from (A):

(C)   If A is an R submodule of a torsionless R module B, then A is torsionless.

Proof.   Look at $\bigcap_{b^* \in B^*} b^*|_A$ and use (B).

(D) A is torsionless if and only if there is an R homomorphism λ such that

$$0 \to A \xrightarrow{\lambda} \prod_{\alpha \in \mathfrak{a}} R_\alpha \qquad R_\alpha = R$$

is exact.

Proof.   Suppose the sequence is exact. Since each R_α is torsionless, the product of the R_α's is also torsionless (the projections on the α component of πR_α is in $(\pi R_\alpha)^*$) and (C) gives the result.

Conversely, suppose A is torsionless. Form

$$\prod_{a^* \in A^*} R_{a^*}$$

and consider $\lambda: A \to \Pi R_a{}^*$, defined by $\lambda(a)[a^*] = a^*$ applied to a. By (B), $\operatorname{Ker} \lambda = (0)$.

In the proof of (D) above, we did not need to embed A in such a large product. That is, if $\{a_\alpha^*\}$ generate A^*, and A is torsionless, then we get the monomorphism $\lambda: A \to \Pi R_\alpha$. Thus, if A^* is finitely generated, and A is torsionless, then A can be embedded in a free and hence projective R module.

(E)   Factors of torsionless modules need not be torsionless, for the group Z is torsionless (in fact, reflexive) and $Z/(n)$ is not torsionless. It is also true (but harder to prove) that extensions of torsionless modules may fail to be torsionless. That is, if A and C are torsionless, there may be nontorsionless B such that $0 \to A \to B \to C \to 0$ is exact.

We should like a duality theory with the properties that duals of projectives are projective and that projectives are reflexive. So, we wish to consider a class of modules with these properties. Also, we shall be considering short exact sequences of these modules (and thereby taking submodules and factor modules in our class). It becomes clear that we must stick to the class of finitely generated modules, and in order to stay in this class when taking submodules, we must require that the rings be Noetherian. Consequently, we shall make the following hypothesis.

Standing Hypothesis. Throughout the remainder of this chapter, every module in sight will be a finitely generated module over a ring that is both right and left Noetherian.

We are then assured that projectives are reflexive and duals of projectives are projective. To see that duals of finitely generated modules are finitely generated, let A be finitely generated and let P be a finitely generated projective such that $\pi: P \to A$ is onto. Then

$$0 \to A^* \xrightarrow{\pi^*} P^*$$

is exact, and since P^* is finitely generated, A^* is also.

Torsionless and Dual Theorem. Let R be both right and left Noetherian; A, a finitely generated R module; B, a finitely generated torsionless R module; and C^*, the dual of a finitely generated R right module C. If any one of the R modules A, B, or C is given, then the other two exist and are connected by the following exact sequences:

$$0 \to C^* \to P \to B \to 0, \tag{5.1}$$

$$0 \to B \to F' \to A \to 0, \tag{5.2}$$

where P and F' are projective R modules.

Proof. Consider (5.1). Let B be a torsionless R module and let $b_1^*, \cdots, b_n^*$ be a set of generators for B^*. Define

$$\lambda: B \to + \sum_{i=1}^{n} R_i = F, \quad R_i = R,$$

by

$$\lambda(b) = (b_1^*(b), \cdots, b_n^*(b)).$$

By property (D) of torsionless modules, λ is a monomorphism. Let $A = F/\operatorname{Im} \lambda$. Then

$$0 \to B \to F \to A \to 0$$

is exact.

Next, suppose A is any R module. Let F be a projective R module mapping onto A, and let B be the kernel of this map. B is torsionless, since it is an R submodule of the free R module F.

To establish the connection between torsionless modules and duals, we use an argument that shows a little more than is claimed by the theorem. Let B be an R module and consider

$$0 \to M \xrightarrow{j} P \xrightarrow{p} B \to 0 \qquad \text{exact,}$$

with P projective. Now dualize to get the short exact sequence

$$0 \to B^* \xrightarrow{\rho^*} P^* \xrightarrow{\pi} C \to 0$$

where $C = P^*/\operatorname{Im} \rho^*$ and π is the natural map. The first thing to note here is that the R module C is always torsionless because, in the exact sequence

$$0 \to B^* \xrightarrow{\rho^*} P^* \xrightarrow{j^*} M^*,$$

C is chosen as $\operatorname{Im} j^*$ in M^*. But M^* is torsionless ("duals are torsionless") and so is any R submodule of it. This shows one part of the connection between torsionless modules and duals. Now star the above sequence and hook it up to the original sequence with σ's to get

$$
\begin{array}{ccccc}
0 \to & C^* & \xrightarrow{\pi^*} & P^{**} & \xrightarrow{\rho^{**}} B^{**} \\
 & \uparrow \tau & & \uparrow \sigma_P & \uparrow \sigma_B \\
0 \to & M & \xrightarrow{j} & P & \xrightarrow{\rho} B \to 0
\end{array}
$$

where τ is defined to make the left square commutative. One should check to see that τ is well defined and that τ is a monomorphism. Also, from the commutativity of the right square and the fact that σ_P is an isomorphism, we get the following equalities:

$$\operatorname{Im} \rho^{**} = \operatorname{Im} \rho^{**}\sigma_P = \operatorname{Im} \sigma_B\rho = \operatorname{Im} \sigma_B,$$

and the diagram can be altered to read

$$
\begin{array}{ccccc}
 & 0 & & 0 & \\
 & \uparrow & & \uparrow & \\
0 \to C^* & \xrightarrow{\pi^*} & P^{**} & \xrightarrow{\rho^{**}} & \operatorname{Im} \sigma_B \to 0 \\
\uparrow \tau & & \uparrow \sigma_P & & \uparrow \sigma_B \\
0 \to M & \xrightarrow{j} & P & \xrightarrow{\rho} & B \quad \to 0 \\
\uparrow & & \uparrow & & \\
0 & & 0 & &
\end{array}
$$

with all columns and rows exact. Now observe that σ_B is a monomorphism if and only if τ is an epimorphism. In fact, the reader can verify that $\operatorname{Ker} \sigma_B = C^*/\operatorname{Im} \tau$.

If B is torsionless, then τ is an isomorphism, and the embedding $0 \to M \xrightarrow{j} P$ can be considered as the dual of the sequence $P^* \xrightarrow{\pi} C \to 0$. Thus, $M = C^*$, a dual.

This completes the proof of the theorem.

Some remarks are in order concerning the theorem. If one starts with an arbitrary A or a torsionless B, absolutely nothing can go wrong. That is, any choice of projective P and P' for which

$$0 \to M \xrightarrow{j} P \to B \to 0$$

and

$$0 \to B \to P' \to A \to 0$$

are exact will ensure that $0 \to M \xrightarrow{j} P$ is really the dual of a sequence $P^* \xrightarrow{\pi} C \to 0$ and that $M = C^*$.

However, given C^*, not every embedding of C^* into a projective will give rise to a torsionless factor module. The theorem shows that a necessary and sufficient condition for the exact sequence

$$0 \to C^* \xrightarrow{i} P \to B \to 0$$

to have B torsionless is that $0 \to C^* \xrightarrow{i} P$ be the dual of an epimorphism $P^* \xrightarrow{\pi} C \to 0$.

As an example, consider

$$0 \to Z \xrightarrow{j} Z \to Z_2 \to 0,$$

where j is multiplication by 2. Of course we have $Z = Z^*$, a dual, but Z_2 is *not* torsionless.

Remark. At this point we invite the reader to examine the complex used in Chapter 3 to define $\text{Ext}^n (A, C)$. If we let $C = R$, the ring, we see that the groups of that complex are now R modules (of the kind opposite from A). Also, the differentiations in that complex are module homomorphisms. Consequently, the groups $\text{Ext}^n (A, R)$ are R modules of the kind opposite from A. Also, it can be shown that all the induced homomorphisms in the first variable become module homomorphisms. Of course $\text{Ext}^0 (A, R)$ has been shortened to A^* in this chapter.

A Duality Theorem. If A is a torsionless R module, there exists a torsionless R right module B such that the sequences

$$0 \to A^* \to \quad P^* \to B \to 0, \qquad (5.3)$$
$$0 \to B^* \to \quad P \to A \to 0, \qquad (5.4)$$
$$0 \to A \to A^{**} \to \text{Ext}^1 (B, R) \to 0, \qquad (5.5)$$

and

$$0 \to B \to B^{**} \to \text{Ext}^1 (A, R) \to 0 \qquad (5.6)$$

are all exact, and where P and P^* are projectives.

Proof. Let P be a projective such that

$$0 \to M \xrightarrow{j} P \xrightarrow{\pi} A \to 0$$

is exact. Then

$$0 \to A^* \xrightarrow{\pi^*} P^* \xrightarrow{\rho} B \to 0$$

is exact and where ρ is the natural map of P^* on $P^*/\mathrm{Im}\,\pi^* = B$. This is (5.3). Next,

$$0 \to B^* \xrightarrow{\rho^*} P^{**} \xrightarrow{\pi^{**}} \mathrm{Im}\,\sigma_A \to 0$$

is exact by the argument in the shifting theorem. Making the appropriate identifications and using $A \cong \mathrm{Im}\,\sigma_A$, we get

$$0 \to B^* \xrightarrow{\rho^*} P \to A \to 0,$$

and this is exact. Notice that B is torsionless by the torsionless and dual theorem and the remark following it.

Having chosen A, the roles of A and B in the above sequences are symmetric. Now star to get

$$0 \to B^* \xrightarrow{\rho^*} P^{**} \xrightarrow{\pi^{**}} A^{**} \to \mathrm{Ext}^1\,(B, R) \to 0$$

from the exact sequence of homology. We note that $\mathrm{Im}\,\pi^{**}$ in A^{**} is $\mathrm{Im}\,\sigma_A$; so, we can construct the short exact sequence

$$0 \to A \xrightarrow{\sigma} A^{**} \to \mathrm{Ext}^1\,(B, R) \to 0.$$

Apply the same process to the other sequence, with the roles of A and B reversed to get the exact sequence

$$0 \to B \xrightarrow{\sigma} B^{**} \to \mathrm{Ext}^1\,(A, R) \to 0.$$

This proves the theorem.

COROLLARY. The following statements are equivalent:

(1) Torsionless R modules are reflexive.
(2) $\mathrm{Ext}^1\,(B, R) = 0$ for all torsionless R right modules B.
(3) $\mathrm{Ext}^2\,(A, R) = 0$ for all R right modules A.
(4) $\mathrm{Id}(R_R) \leq 1$.

Proof. (1) is equivalent to (2) by the duality theorem. The equivalence of (2) and (3) comes from the torsionless and duality theorem and the exact sequence of homology. The fact that (3) is equivalent to (4) follows from the injective dimension theorem of the preceding chapter.

COROLLARY. The following statements are equivalent:

(1) C^* is reflexive for every R module C.
(2) $[\mathrm{Ext}^1\,(B, R)]^* = 0$ for all torsionless R right modules B.
(3) $[\mathrm{Ext}^2\,(A, R)]^* = 0$ for all R right modules A.

Proof. Look at

$$0 \to C \to C^{**} \to \mathrm{Ext}^1 (B, R) \to 0$$

and

$$0 \to [\mathrm{Ext}^1 (B, R)]^* \to C^{***} \to C^* \to 0,$$

the latter sequence being split exact. Again (2) and (3) are equivalent by the torsionless and duality theorem.

The following theorem enables us to solve the equation $A = \mathrm{Ext}^n (X, R)$ for X in the case that $A^* = 0$.

THEOREM. If A is an R right module such that $A^* = 0$, then there exists an R right module B such that $A = \mathrm{Ext}^1 (B, R)$. Moreover, one can choose B so that $Pd(B) = 1$ if $A \neq 0$.

Proof. If $A = 0$, then B may be taken to be any projective. Hence, assume $A \neq 0$. Start to resolve A:

$$P_1 \xrightarrow{d} P_0 \xrightarrow{\epsilon} A \to 0,$$

and form the exact sequence

$$0 \to A^* \xrightarrow{\epsilon^*} P_0^* \xrightarrow{d^*} P_1^* \to B \to 0,$$

where $B = P_1^*/\mathrm{Im}\ d^*$. Since $A^* = 0$, we obtain the exact sequence

$$0 \to P_0^* \xrightarrow{d^*} P_1^* \to B \to 0.$$

Note that we can now conclude $Pd(B) \leq 1$. Form the diagram

$$
\begin{array}{ccccccccc}
0 \to B^* \to & P_1^{**} & \xrightarrow{d^{**}} & P_0^{**} & \to & \mathrm{Ext}^1 (B, R) & \to \mathrm{Ext}^1 (P_1^*, R) = 0 \\
& \uparrow \sigma & & \uparrow \sigma & & \uparrow \rho & \\
& P_1 & \xrightarrow{d} & P_0 \to A & & \to 0. &
\end{array}
$$

Since each of the σ's is an isomorphism, so is ρ; that is,

$$0 \neq A = \mathrm{Ext}^1 (B, R).$$

This implies that $Pd(B) \geq 1$. Hence the theorem is proved. As a partial converse to this theorem we have the next theorem.

THEOREM. If $Pd(B) = 1$, then $[\mathrm{Ext}^1 (B, R)]^* = 0$.

Proof. Resolve B:

$$0 \to P_1 \xrightarrow{d} P_0 \to B \to 0.$$

Use this to form

$$0 \to B^* \to P_0^* \xrightarrow{d^*} P_1^* \xrightarrow{\theta} \text{Ext}^1 (B, R) \to 0$$

and the commutative diagram with exact rows

$$0 \to [\text{Ext}^1 (B, R)]^* \xrightarrow{\theta^*} P_1^{**} \xrightarrow{d^{**}} P_0^{**}$$
$$\uparrow \sigma \qquad\qquad \uparrow \sigma$$
$$0 \qquad \to P_1 \xrightarrow{d} P_0.$$

Notice that the two σ's are isomorphisms and d is a monomorphism; hence, d^{**} is a monomorphism. It follows that $[\text{Ext}^1 (B, R)]^* = 0$.

The above theorem allows us to gather a bit of information concerning the finitistic dimension in the case that dimension is small. Recall the definition:

$$LfPD(R) = \sup Pd(A) | A \text{ finitely generated}, \qquad Pd(A) < \infty.$$

COROLLARY. $LfPD(R) = 0$ if and only if every nonzero R right module A has nonzero dual.

Proof. Let $LfPD(R) = 0$. Suppose A $(A \neq 0)$ is an R right module such that $A^* = 0$. Then there is a B such that $Pd(B) = 1$, contrary to hypothesis. Conversely, if $LfPD(R) \neq 0$, then there is a B such that $Pd(B) = 1$. Let $A = \text{Ext}^1 (B, R)$ and the preceding theorem shows $A^* = 0$. It remains to be shown that $A \neq 0$, which we leave to the reader. See exercise 8 at the end of this chapter.

THEOREM. The following statements are equivalent:

(1) $LfPD(R) \leq 1$.

(2) Torsionless R modules have projective dimension either zero or infinity.

(3) If A is a torsionless R right module such that A^* is projective, then A is projective.

Proof. (1) is equivalent to (2) by the torsionless and dual theorem. It is therefore sufficient to show that (2) is equivalent to (3).

Assume (2) and let A be a torsionless R right module whose dual A^* is projective. By the duality theorem, we have exact sequences

$$0 \to B^* \to P \xrightarrow{\pi} A \to 0$$

and

$$0 \to A^* \xrightarrow{\pi^*} P^* \to B \to 0.$$

Now (2) implies that the bottom sequence is split exact, and the induced map

$$P^{**} \xrightarrow{\pi^{**}} A^{**}$$

is a split epimorphism (that is, the dual sequence is exact and split). But from the proof of the torsionless and dual theorem $\operatorname{Im} \pi^{**} = \operatorname{Im} \sigma_A$, and this latter is A, since A was assumed torsionless. Hence, A is projective.

Conversely, assume (3) and let B be a torsionless R module of projective dimension exactly 1. We shall show that this implies a contradiction. Note that if there are any torsionless modules of finite (but nonzero) projective dimension, then there is one of dimension exactly 1. According to the duality theorem, we have

$$0 \to A^* \to P \xrightarrow{\pi} B \to 0$$

and

$$0 \to B^* \xrightarrow{\pi^*} P^* \to A \to 0,$$

where A is a torsionless R right module with a projective dual A^*. By (3) the lower sequence is split exact (A is projective). But then, reasoning as above, $\operatorname{Im} \pi^{**} = B$ is also projective, which contradicts the assumption that it had dimension exactly 1.

One of the corollaries to the duality theorem gives a connection between duality and the injective dimension of $_RR$. This might lead one to ask what sort of rings have the property that injective dimension of $_RR$ is 0. Clearly, this is equivalent to the vanishing of $\operatorname{Ext}^1(A, R)$ for all R modules A, and this in turn is equivalent to the statement, "The duals of short exact sequences are short exact sequences." In the following discussion, we shall study rings with these properties and we shall show that these rings have a number of remarkable properties. They have been studied for many years by a number of authors. This is a good place for the definition of these rings.

DEFINITION. A left and right Noetherian ring R that is left self-injective ($_RR$ is injective) will be called a quasi-Frobenius (QF) ring.

Note that the definition is not left-right symmetric. However, we shall show eventually that a QF ring is also right self-injective (and has many other properties).

We proceed with a series of technical lemmas that list some of the properties of QF rings.

Lemma 1. If R is a QF ring and if $0 \to X \to Y \to Z \to 0$ is a short exact sequence of right modules, then it can be embedded in the commutative diagram

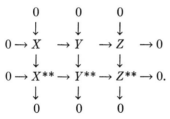

Proof. Another way to phrase the lemma is to say that (**) is an exact functor on finitely generated right modules and is equivalent to the identity functor. To prove the lemma, we first show that right modules are reflexive. If X is a right module, we form the sequence of right modules,

$$0 \to M \xrightarrow{\rho} P \to X \to 0$$

where P is projective and M is torsionless. Since R is left self-injective, M is reflexive (the duality theorem and the fact that $\text{Ext}^1(B, R) = 0$ for left modules B). Form the exact squencee of modules

$$0 \to X^* \to P^* \xrightarrow{\rho^*} M^*.$$

Now star this sequence, using the fact that $\text{Hom}_R(\cdot_R R)$ is an *exact* functor. We obtain the commutative exact diagram:

$$
\begin{array}{ccccccc}
& 0 & & 0 & & & \\
& \uparrow & & \uparrow & & & \\
M^{**} & \xrightarrow{\rho^{**}} & P^{**} & \to & X^{**} & \to & 0 \\
\sigma_M \uparrow & & \sigma_P \uparrow & & \uparrow \sigma_X & & \\
0 \to M & \to & P & \to & X & \to & 0. \\
\uparrow & & \uparrow & & & & \\
0 & & 0 & & & &
\end{array}
$$

By chasing the diagram, we see that ρ^{**} must be a monomorphism. This, in turn, forces σ_X to be an isomorphism.

Now we turn to the more general case of the sequence of finitely generated right modules:

$$0 \to X \to Y \to Z \to 0.$$

Star it once to obtain

$$0 \to Z^* \to Y^* \to X^*,$$

an exact sequence of left modules. The star applied to this is an exact functor. and gives the following exact commutative diagram:

$$
\begin{array}{ccccccc}
0 & & 0 & & 0 & & \\
\downarrow & & \downarrow & & \downarrow & & \\
0 \to X & \to & Y & \to & Z & \to & 0 \\
\downarrow & & \downarrow & & \downarrow & & \\
X^{**} & \to & Y^{**} & \to & Z^{**} & \to & 0. \\
\downarrow & & \downarrow & & \downarrow & & \\
0 & & 0 & & 0 & &
\end{array}
$$

But diagram chasing allows us to put a zero in the lower left-hand corner. This completes the proof of the lemma.

Lemma 2. If R is a QF ring, then R has minimum condition on right ideals.

Proof. If H, K are two unequal right ideals with $H \subset K$, then we have the diagram

$$
\begin{array}{ccccccc}
& & 0 & & & & \\
& & \downarrow & & & & \\
0 \to & H & \to R \to & R/H & \to 0 & & \\
& \downarrow & & \downarrow \mu & & & \\
0 \to & K & \to R \to & R/K & \to 0, & & \\
& & \downarrow & & & & \\
& & 0 & & & &
\end{array}
$$

where the map μ of R/H on R/K is not an isomorphism. This induces the exact diagram

$$
\begin{array}{ccc}
0 \to (R/H)^* \to R^* \\
\quad {}^{\mu^*}\uparrow \\
0 \to (R/K)^* \to R^*, \\
\uparrow \\
0
\end{array}
$$

where $(R/K)^*$ and $(R/H)^*$ are left ideals in R. The claim is that the monomorphism μ^* of $(R/K)^*$ into $(R/H)^*$ cannot be an isomorphism, for if it were, it would induce an isomorphism $(R/H)^{**} \xrightarrow{\mu^{**}} (R/K)^{**}$. But, by Lemma 1, we have this exact diagram:

$$
\begin{array}{ccc}
0 & & 0 \\
\downarrow & & \downarrow \\
R/H & \xrightarrow{\mu} & R/K \quad \to 0 \\
\downarrow & & \downarrow \\
0 \to (R/H)^{**} & \xrightarrow{\mu^{**}} & (R/K)^{**} \to 0 \\
\downarrow & & \downarrow \\
0 & & 0
\end{array}
$$

This means that μ is an isomorphism contrary to the hypothesis.

Now suppose that $\{H_\alpha\}$ is a collection of right ideals of R that does not have a minimal element. Then, by the first part of the proof, the collection $\{R/H_\alpha\}^*$ does not have a maximal element, which contradicts the assumption that R is left Noetherian. Hence, R must have minimum condition on right ideals.

Now that we know that QF rings have minimum condition on right ideals, we can recall a few facts about such rings, which we shall need in the proof of the next theorem. Some of these facts are in the exercises at the end of Chapter 2 (although they are stated there for left ideals). Those readers who have not been doing their homework may find it necessary to go back and do these exercises now.

If R has minimum condition on right ideals, then R contains a nilpotent ideal N (the radical of R) such that R/N is a semisimple ring with minimum condition (Exercises 7–16, Chapter 2).

If S is a simple R module, then we see that $NS = 0$ because NS is a submodule of S; if $NS = S$ (the only other possibility when S is simple), then $N^r S = S$ for all r. But, since N is nilpotent, $N^r = 0$ for large enough r, so $S = 0$, contradicting the assumption that S is simple. The same argument works for simple *right* R-modules T, that is, $TN = 0$.

Thus we see that if R has minimum condition on right ideals, the simple R-modules are really R/N modules. But we know from the structure theorem for semisimple rings with minimum condition that R/N has the same (finite) number of simple left modules as simple right modules, counting isomorphic ones as the same. But this statement also holds for simple R modules (see Exercise 16, Chapter 2).

One more fact we need concerning rings with minimum condition on right ideals is that every nonzero left ideal contains a simple left ideal. Note that we do not yet claim that R has minimum condition on left ideals. Let L be a left ideal and examine the descending chain $L \supseteq NL \supseteq N^2L \cdots N^rL = 0$. For some i, we see that $N^{i-1}L \neq 0$ and $N^iL = 0$. But then $N^{i-1}L$ is an R/N module, and by the structure theorem for such modules, $N^{i-1}L$ is the direct sum of simple R/N modules. Any one of these is the desired simple left ideal in L.

The above facts concerning rings with minimum condition on right ideals are enough to enable us to prove the next theorem.

THEOREM.   If R is a QF ring, then R is right self-injective.

Proof.   The idea of the proof is to first show that for nonzero left modules A, $A^* \neq 0$. After this has been demonstrated, it is fairly easy to show that R is right self-injective.

Let A be a nonzero, finitely generated, left R module. Since A is Noetherian, A has a maximal submodule B such that A/B is simple. We shall be able to show that $A^* \neq 0$ if we can show that the simple module A/B is isomorphic to a left ideal of R; for, this gives a nonzero homomorphism of A into R.

Therefore, it is enough to show that every simple left R module is isomorphic to a left ideal of R. We shall do this by a counting argument. Since we know that R has minimum condition on right ideals, we know that R

has as many simple left modules as simple right modules. What we shall show is that for every simple right module T, there exists a simple left ideal $S(T)$ of R such that if $S(T) = S(T')$, then $T = T'$. This is sufficient to show that every simple left module is isomorphic to a simple left ideal.

Let T be a simple right module. Then $0 \to H \to R \xrightarrow{\nu} T \to 0$ is exact, and this induces $0 \to T^* \xrightarrow{\nu^*} R^*$ exact. T^* is not zero because right modules are reflexive. T^* is a left ideal of R, and by the remarks preceding the theorem, T^* contains a simple left ideal $S(T)$. We claim that $[S(T)]^* = T^{**} = T$; for, we have the exact diagram of left modules,

$$
\begin{array}{ccc}
0 \to & T^* \xrightarrow{\nu^*} & R \\
& \scriptstyle{j} \uparrow & \\
0 \to & S(T) \to & R, \\
& \uparrow & \\
& 0 &
\end{array}
$$

which remains exact when starred:

$$
\begin{array}{ccc}
R \xrightarrow{\nu^{**}} & T^{**} \to 0 \\
& \downarrow \scriptstyle{j^*} \\
R \to & (S(T))^* \to 0. \\
& \downarrow \\
& 0
\end{array}
$$

But $T^{**} \cong T$ is simple; so, j^* is either an isomorphism or the zero map. It cannot be the zero map unless $(S(T))^* = 0$. But $S(T)$ is a left ideal of R and is therefore torsionless. Thus, we have shown that $(S(T))^* = T$.

We now know that every simple left module must appear as a left ideal and that if $0 \neq A$ is a left R module, then $A^* \neq 0$.

We now proceed to show that R is right self-injective. By the injective dimension theorem, it is enough to show that $\text{Ext}^1 (R/H, R) = 0$ for right ideals H of R. From the sequence

$$0 \to H \xrightarrow{i} R \to R/H \to 0,$$

we obtain

$$0 \to (R/H)^* \to R^{*j*} \to H^* \to \text{Ext}^1 (R/H, R) \to 0,$$

an exact sequence of left modules. Now star again to obtain the exact sequence of right modules:

$$0 \to [\text{Ext}^1 (R/H, R)]^* \to H^{**} \xrightarrow{j^{**}} R^{**}.$$

But j^{**} is a monomorphism by Lemma 1; so, $[\text{Ext}^1 (R/H, R)]^* = 0$. But this implies, by the first part of the proof, that $\text{Ext}^1 (R/H, R) = 0$, and the proof of the theorem has been completed.

In the following theorem, we sum up the main properties of the QF rings that we have developed.

QF Theorem. If R is both left and right Noetherian, then the following properties are equivalent:

(1) R is QF.
(2) (*) is an exact functor on finitely generated left modules.
(3) $\text{Ext}^1 (A, R) = 0$ for all left modules A.
(4) $_R R$ is injective.
(5) Every projective left module is injective.
(6) R has minimum condition on left ideals and on right ideals and is both left and right self-injective.

Proof. Properties (2), (3), and (4) are equivalent by the injective dimension theorem. Of course (1) and (4) are equivalent by the definition of QF rings.

Clearly, (5) implies (4). We show that (4) implies (5). It is enough to show that free modules are injective because projectives are direct summands of free modules and will be injective if the free modules are. Let $F = + \sum R$ be a free module and examine the diagram

$$0 \to L \to R$$
$$f \downarrow$$
$$F$$

where L is a left ideal. Note that, since L is finitely generated, Im f is contained in a free, finitely generated, direct summand F' of F; and F', being the direct sum of a finite number of copies of R, is injective. Thus the preceding diagram can be embedded in a commutative diagram,

$$0 \to L \to R$$
$$f \downarrow \quad g \diagup \qquad ,$$
$$F$$

where g is really a homomorphism into $F' \subseteq F$. Hence, F is injective by the injective test theorem.

To show (1) → (6), the preceding theorem shows that R is right self-injective, and Lemma 2 shows that R has minimum condition on right ideals. But as soon as we know that R is right self-injective, the proof of Lemma 2 with right and left interchanged shows that R has minimum condition on left ideals. This completes the proof of the QF theorem.

Note in the preceding theorem that (6) is left and right symmetric; therefore the same properties hold with left and right interchanged.

EXERCISES

Assume the ring R is both left and right Noetherian and all R-modules are finitely generated.

1. DEFINITION. An R module M is called a W *module* if $\text{Ext}^1(M, R) = 0$. Prove that the following conditions are equivalent:
   (a) All left W modules are torsionless.
   (b) All right torsionless modules are W modules.
   (c) All torsionless left modules are reflexive.

2. For the rings under consideration, prove that the following are equivalent:
   (a) All left W modules are projective.
   (b) l.gl.dim. $R \leq 1$.

3. From now on let R be a Noetherian integral domain (commutative Noetherian, and no zero divisors). We shall say that the rank of a module M is the cardinality of the basis of "the largest" free submodule of M (largest in the sense of having the largest basis); denote it by $r(M)$. From this definition, deduce that if T is a submodule of M, then $r(T) \leq r(M)$.

4. Show that the rank of a finitely generated module is finite.

5. Use Exercise 3 to show the following properties:
   (a) $r(M) \geq r(M^*)$ for torsionless M.
   (b) Duals are reflexive.
   (c) $[\text{Ext}^1(B, R)]^* = 0$ for all torsionless B.
   (d) $[\text{Ext}^2(A, R)]^* = 0$ for all A.

6. Suppose that $Pd(A) = n$; show that there exists F free, such that $\text{Ext}^n(A, F) \neq 0$.

7. Let R be left Noetherian and A be the finitely generated R module. Show that $Pd(A) = n$ if and only if $\text{Ext}^{n+1}(A, C) = 0$ for all finitely generated R modules C. (HINT. Use a finitely generated resolution of A.)

8. Again with A finitely generated and R left Noetherian, show that if $Pd(A) = n$, then $\text{Ext}^n(A, R) \neq 0$.

9. Consider the ring R of matrices with coefficients in a field F of the form

$$\begin{matrix} x & 0 & 0 \\ y & x & 0 \\ z & 0 & x \end{matrix}$$

Show that the radical N of the commutative ring R is the set of elements with $x = 0$. Form $(R/N)^* \cdots ^*$ (n stars) and show that these have vector-space dimension 2^n over the field F. Are duals always reflexive?

10. Let A be an algebra over a field K with $[A:K] = n$. Show that if P is a finitely generated, A-projective module, then $\text{Hom}_K(P, K)$ is a finitely

generated, A-injective (right) module. Show that every finitely generated, right A-injective module is so obtained.

11. Prove that over the integers there are no finitely generated injectives (except 0).

The following objects can be defined in any ring. Let S be a subset of R and define $r(S) = \{x|Sx = 0\}$ and $l(S) = \{y|yS = 0\}$, the right and left annihilators of S.

12. Prove the following:
   (a) If $S \subseteq T$, then $l(S) \supseteq l(T)$ and $r(S) \supseteq r(T)$.
   (b) $l(S)$ is always a left ideal and $r(S)$ is a right ideal.
   (c) If L is a left ideal, then $r(L) = (R/L)^*$.

We shall say that a ring satisfies the *annihilator conditions* if $l(r(L)) = L$ and $r(l(H)) = H$ for all left ideals L and right ideals H.

13. Prove that if R satisfies the annihilator conditions and if R is left Noetherian, then R has minimum condition on right ideals.

14. Prove that if R satisfies the annihilator conditions and any one of the conditions — left Noetherian, right Noetherian, minimum condition on right ideals, minimum condition on left ideals — then it satisfies all four conditions.

15. Prove that R is QF if and only if R has one of the four conditions listed in Exercise 14 and satisfies the annihilator conditions.

16. Prove the following theorem. If R is left Noetherian, then R is a QF ring if and only if every finitely generated module is reflexive.

Let R be an algebra over a field K and suppose that $[R:K] = n < \infty$. We shall say that such an algebra is a Frobenius algebra if the two R modules $\mathrm{Hom}_K (R_R, K)$ and $_RR$ are isomorphic. Recall that for f in $\mathrm{Hom}_K (R_R, K)$, $(rf)(x) = f(xr)$. This makes $\mathrm{Hom}_K (R_R, K)$ into a left R module.

17. Prove that a Frobenius algebra is a QF ring. Exercise 10 may help.

18. Let R be any algebra over a field K with $[R:K] = n < \infty$. Prove $\mathrm{Hom}_R (_RR, \mathrm{Hom}_K (R_R, K)) \cong \mathrm{Hom}_K (R, K)$. HINT. If $\mu : {}_RR \to \mathrm{Hom}_K (R_R, K)$ is a left R homomorphism, let $\beta(r)$ be "$\mu(1)$ applied to r" and check the properties of β. Then reverse the process.

19. Prove that an algebra R over K is Frobenius if and only if there exists β in $\mathrm{Hom}_K (R, K)$ such that $\mathrm{Ker}\, \beta$ contains no left and no right ideals except zero.

20. Let R be the group algebra of a finite group G over the field K. Prove that R is a Frobenius algebra. HINT. Let $\beta(r)$ be the coefficient of 1 in r.

21. Give an example of a QF ring that is not a semisimple ring.

References

In the pursuit of more ring structure, one can go in several directions. For instance, one can cast off the various finiteness conditions and see what happens in more general rings. A good source of material on this is Jacobson's *Structure of Rings* [Ref. 17]. One should note that all of Chapter 3 and most of Chapter 4 apply to rings without any finiteness conditions.

One may keep minimum condition and classify the rings in more detail. See Refs. 15, 16, 27, 28, 33, and 34 for generalizations of semisimple, QF, Frobenius algebras, and the various concepts we introduced in Chapters 2 and 5. Another direction in which one can go is to commutative Noetherian rings. There appear to be lots of connections between the concepts of classical ideal theory and some of the homological ideas [Refs. 4, 5, 29, 32].

For various duality theories, try Refs. 8, 22, 25, 26. Our development of QF rings is adapted largely from Ref. 8.

There are numerous papers on projective dimension and various other dimensions that we have not mentioned [Refs. 2, 3, 6, 10, 11, 12, 14, 18, 21, 23, 29]. Many of the unsolved problems appear to be connected with the finitistic dimensions. Bass [Ref. 6] is a good source of the latest results in this direction.

There are several papers concerned with the structure of projective and injective modules over various rings [Refs. 9, 19, 24, 26].

For more homological algebra, one might consult one of the three standard texts, Northcott [Ref. 30], Cartan and Eilenberg [Ref. 7]. MacLane [Ref. 35]. Although we feel that we have done a reasonably complete job on Ext, this is only about one third of homological algebra. In order to be properly educated, one really needs the tensor product and Tor and some of the relations between these functors and Ext.

The following list includes papers and books to which we have referred.

1. Artin, E., C. Nesbitt, and R. Thrall, *Rings with Minimum Condition*. Ann Arbor: University of Michigan Press, 1944.

2. Auslander, M., "On the dimension of modules and algebras. VI. Comparison of global and algebra dimension," *Nagoya Math. J.*, vol. 11 (1957), pp. 61–65.

3. Auslander, M., "On the dimension of modules and algebras. III. Global dimension," *Nagoya Math. J.*, vol. 9 (1955), pp. 67–77.

4. Auslander, M., and D. A. Buchsbaum, "Homological dimension in Noetherian rings," *Trans. Amer. Math. Soc.*, vol. 85 (1957), pp. 390–405.

5. Auslander, M., and D. A. Buchsbaum, "Homological dimension in Noetherian Rings. II," *Trans. Amer. Math. Soc.*, vol. 88 (1958), pp. 194–206.

6. Bass, H., "Finitistic dimension and a homological generalization of semi-primary rings," *Trans. Amer. Math. Soc.*, vol. 95 (1960), pp. 466–488.

7. Cartan, H., and S. Eilenberg, *Homological Algebra*. Princeton: Princeton University Press, 1956.

8. Dieudonne, J., "Remarks on quasi-Frobenius rings. III," *J. Math.*, vol. 2 (1958), pp. 346–354.

9. Eckmann, B., and A. Schopf, "Uber injective moduln," *Arch. Math.*, vol. 4 (1953), pp. 75–78.

10. Eilenberg, S., M. Ikeda, and T. Nakayama, "On the dimension of modules and algebras. I," *Nagoya Math. J.*, vol. 8 (1955), pp. 49–57.

11. Eilenberg, S., H. Nagao, and T. Nakayama, "On the dimension of modules and algebras. IV. Dimension of residue rings of hereditary rings," *Nagoya Math. J.*, vol. 10 (1956), pp. 87–95.

12. Eilenberg, S., and T. Nakayama, "On the dimension of modules and algebras. V. Dimension of residue rings," *Nagoya Math. J.*, vol. 11 (1957), pp. 9–12.

13. Eilenberg, S., and T. Nakayama, "On the dimension of modules and algebras. II. Frobenius algebras and quasi-Frobenius rings," *Nagoya Math. J.*, vol. 9 (1955), pp. 1–16.

14. Eilenberg, S., A. Rosenberg, and D. Zelinsky, "On the dimension of modules and algebras. VIII. Dimension of tensor products," *Nagoya Math. J.*, vol. 12 (1957), pp. 71–93.

15. Ikeda, M., "Some generalizations of quasi-Frobenius rings," *Osaka Math. J.*, vol. 12 (1957), pp. 71–93.

16. Ikeda, M., and T. Nakayama, "Supplementary remarks on Frobenius algebras. II," *Osaka Math. J.*, vol. 2 (1950), pp. 7–12.

17. Jacobson, N., *Structure of Rings*. New York: Amer. Math. Soc., Coll. Publ., Vol. 37.

18. Jans, J. P., and T. Nakayama, "On the dimension of modules and algebras. VII. Algebras with finite-dimensional residue algebras," *Nagoya Math. J.*, vol. 11 (1957), pp. 67–76.

19. Jans, J. P., "Projective injective modules," *Pacific J. of Math.*, vol. 9 (1959), pp. 1103–1108.

20. Jans, J. P., "Some remarks on symmetric and Frobenius algebras," *Nagoya Math. J.*, vol. 16 (1960), pp. 65–71.

21. Jans, J. P., "Some generalizations of finite projective dimension," *Illinois J. Math.*, vol. 5 (1961), pp. 334–344.

22. Jans, J. P., "Duality in Noetherian Rings," *Proc. Amer. Math. Soc.*, vol. 12 (1961), pp. 829–835.

23. Kaplansky, I., "On the dimension of modules and algebras. X. A right hereditary ring which is not left hereditary," *Nagoya Math. J.*, vol. 13 (1958), pp. 85–88.

24. Kaplansky, I., "Projective modules," *Ann. of Math.*, vol. 68, no. 2 (1958), pp. 372–377.

25. Morita, K., "Duality for modules and its applications to the theory of rings with minimum condition," Science Reports, *Tokyo Kyoiku Daigaku*, vol. 6 (1958), pp. 83–142.

26. Morita, K., Y. Kawada, and H. Tachikawa, "On injective modules," *Math. Z.*, vol. 68 (1957), pp. 217–226.

27. Nakayama, T., "On Frobenius algebras. I," *Annals of Math.*, vol. 40 (1939), pp. 611–633.

28. Nakayama, T., "On Frobenius algebras. II," *Annals of Math.*, vol. 42 (1941), pp. 1–21.

29. Northcott, D. G., "A note on the global dimension of polynomial rings," *Proc. Cambridge Philos. Soc.*, vol. 53 (1957), pp. 796–799.

30. Northcott, D. B., *An Introduction to Homological Algebra.* New York: Cambridge University Press, 1960.

31. Nunke, R. J., "Modules of extensions over Dedekind rings," *Illinois J. Math.*, vol. 3 (1959), pp. 224–241.

32. Rees, D., "Polar modules," *Proc. Cambridge Philos. Soc.*, vol. 53 (1957), pp. 554–567.

33. Thrall, R. M., "Some generalizations of quasi-Frobenius algebras," *Trans. Am. Math. Soc.*, vol. 64 (1948), pp. 173–183.

34. Wall, D. W., "Characterizations of generalized uniserial algebras. I," *Trans. Am. Math. Soc.*, vol. 90 (1959), pp. 161–170.

35. MacLane S., *Homology.* New York, Berlin, Göttingen, and Heideberg: Springer, 1963.

Index

Annihilator conditions, 82

Basis of a free module, 7

Complex, 27
Complex map, 27
Composition series, 25
Connecting maps, 28
Cyclic module, 2
Cyclics injectives and Ext corollary, 50

Differentials, 27
Dimension theorem, 48
Direct sum, 5
Divisible group, 51
Division ring, 4
Dual of a module, 65
Duality theorem, 71

Epimorphism, 3
Exact sequence, 6
  of complexes, 28
  in Ext, 41, 42
  of homology theorem, 28
$Ext^n (A, C)$, 33

Factor module, 2
Finitely generated, 2
Finitistic dimensions, 48
Free module, 7
Frobenius algebra, 82
Functor, 37

Generated, 2
Global dimension, 48
Global dimension theorem, 55
Group algebra, 24

$Hom_R (A, B)$, 31
Homological, 11
Homology groups, 27
Homomorphism, 2

Image, 3
Injective dimension, 55
Injective dimension theorem, 55
Injective module, 10, 33
Injective producing lemma, 52
Injective resolution, 54
Injective test theorem, 49
Isomorphism, 3

Kernel, 3

Minimum condition, 10
Module, 1
Monomorphism, 3

Nilpotent, 22
Noetherian, 57

Product, 4
Projective dimension, 48
Projective module, 7, 33
Projective resolution, 33

QF theorem, 80
Quasi-Frobenius (QF) ring, 75
Quotient module, 2

Radical, 26
Reflexive, 65
Right module, 1

s field, 4
Schur's lemma, 4
Semisimple rings with minimum condition, 12
Shifting theorem, 47
   for injectives, 54
Short exact sequence, 6
Simple module, 2
Splitting, 6
   of Ext, 43
Sticky point, 61
Submodule, 2

Third dual theorem, 67
Torsionless, 65
   and dual theorem, 69

Uniqueness theorems, 19, 21

W module, 81

Zorn's lemma, 10